Other New and Natural Titles

NEW & NATURAL

Herbs & Spices

Sonia Allison

BELL & HYMAN

First published 1985 by
Bell & Hyman Limited
Denmark House
37-39 Queen Elizabeth Street
London SE1 2QB

Cover design by Norman Reynolds
Illustrations by Paul Saunders

ISBN 0 7135 2526 6

British Library Cataloguing in Publication Data
Allison, Sonia
Herbs & Spices
I. Cookery (Spices)
I. Title
641.6'383   TX819.A1

Typeset by Typecast Ltd.

Printed and bound
in Great Britain at the Bath Press, Avon

CONTENTS

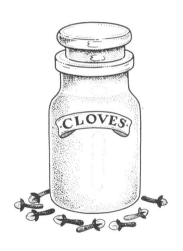

Introduction

There is something splendidly exotic about cooking with herbs and spices since they add a new dimension of flavour to any dish to which they are added. Mixed spice, cinnamon and ground ginger are spices we tend to take for granted; likewise, herbs such as chives, parsley and mint. Yet there are many many more available to us, fresh or dried, to use in cooking and give our food an individual style and taste which, without adornment, would seem singularly bland. The whole ethos of Oriental cuisine is based on the subtle use of assorted spices and finely chosen herbs, and Westerners are now emulating the East and making inroads into the fine art of seasoning by using a wider variety than ever before of herbs and spices from far and wide. Pots and jars jostle for shelf space in the kitchen and even major supermarket chains are showing a spirit of adventure as they introduce more fresh herbs to their customers and provide an ever-increasing range of both familiar and unusual spices.

I have decided to leave the ancient, fascinating and at times mystical history of herbs and spices to the experts, of which there are a great number, while I concentrate on recipes. However, for quick reference and also interest, I give brief details of the herbs and spices used throughout the book, together with a few extra ones should you wish to substitute or experiment with your own combination of flavours. But first, a few generalizations on the differences between the two. Herbs are leafy or flowering plants, sometimes yielding edible seeds, buds and roots, which are available fresh or dried. Many are grown in the UK, Europe and further afield and lend a mild and subtle taste to foods. It may be useful to know that four level teaspoons of chopped fresh herbs equals one teaspoon of the more powerful dried. Spices usually comes from the Orient or other tropical and sub-tropical areas of the world and are available dried, either in ground form or as pieces of bark, root, berries (junipers) and buds (cloves). They are all distinctively pungent and should therefore be used judiciously.

Acknowledgements
The Pasta Information Centre (facing pages 24 and 48).
The Danish Dairy Board (facing page 25).
Schwarz Limited (facing page 49).

Herbs

Basil

A herb native to India and Iran, basil is now grown widely all over Europe though flourishes best in warm climates. Its name comes from the Greek meaning King and its origins are ancient. Related to the mint family and also known as sweet basil, the herb has long slim leaves (up to 1 inch or 3cm in length) with tender stems. Basil is deepish green but dulls down to a brownish colour when dried. It has a mild yet pungent flavour and because of its affinity with tomato dishes, is widely used in Italian cooking. In France, basil is known as the royal herb and is treated with respect. In addition to tomato dishes, basil enhances the flavour of lamb, omelettes and green beans.

Bay Leaves

Grown on ever green laurel bushes and held in high esteem by the ancient Greeks and Romans, the bay leaf is a herb native to the areas around the Mediterranean and is also grown in Mexico and Europe. The fresh and shining deep green leaves can grow up to 3 inches (7.5cm) in length and have an unmistakable flavour and smell. They are widely used in all manner of pickles, marinades and meat stews. When dried, they become brownish in colour and brittle.

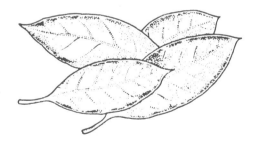

Borage

With long and pointed fleshy leaves in greeny-grey, borage was known and admired by the ancient Greeks and Romans but its origins remain obscure. It is an annual herb which bears lovely blue flowers, preserved and candied during the 18th and 19th centuries. With its faint taste of cucumber, borage is the traditional herb to add to Pimm's No. 1, but serves equally well in other fruit cups and cold punches.

Caraway Seeds

Used to flavour the liqueur known as Kümmel, caraway seeds are native to Europe and grow profusely in Holland. The seeds are the off-spring of a biennial plant belonging to the parsley family and are short and curvy, light brown in colour, very hard and pointed at both ends. They have an unmistakable taste of their own and go well in rye bread, sauerkraut, North and Mid-European stews, Hungary's Goulash and Old English seed cake. Caraway seeds are also used in pickles.

Chervil

Chervil is a herb native to Asia but now grows in all temperate countries of the world. Its leaves are small and green, similar in taste to parsley and best used fresh. The herb is useful for flavouring mild dishes of chicken and veal, and may also be used in egg dishes, soups, salads and selected sauces.

Chives

Grass-like to look at, chives are related to the onion family with a similar taste. They settle and grow almost anywhere and are used both as a flavouring and a garnish. They are a hardy perennial which bear attractive mauve flowers.

Coriander (Fresh)

Native to Asia, Southern Europe and the Middle East, coriander is a member of the parsley family and used just as widely in India, China, Japan and Central and South America as parsley is used in the West. It has a unique flavour and is also known as Chinese parsley, dizzycorn and cilantro and is available in the UK from Greek and Greek Cypriot food shops, as well as Indian and Chinese. The flat, delicate-coloured green leaves and stalks should both be used as an additive for flavouring, the leaves only for garnish. The herb does not take readily to drying and is best used fresh.

Dill

Native to Southern Europe and the Middle East, dill is now grown widely in all temperate countries and is a delicate herb to match the subtlety of mild fish. The word dill is said to come from the Norse 'dilla', to lull, and once thought to induce sleep. It is a fern-like herb, very popular in Northern Europe, Scandinavia, Turkey and Greece. In Britain, it tends to grow wild in the country and cliff tops in Jersey abound with clumps of fragrant dill. It is a natural mate for cucumber and is also companionable in potato salad. Dill seeds, as well as the fresh herb, can be used in pickling.

Garlic

Supposedly given to Egyptian pyramid workers for good health, garlic is native to Asia but is now grown worldwide and is a perennial member of the onion family. Much appreciated in Britain during the reign of Queen Elizabeth the First, garlic is an essential, almost, of Southern and Eastern cooking and has a strong flavour which is liked or not. It grows in bulbs, sometimes wild like dill, each containing individual cloves or segments with their own layers of protective skin.

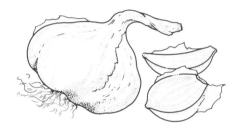

Horseradish

Native to the Far East and Eastern Europe, horseradish is much cultivated in temperate zones of the world. It has a brown, cylindrical root, like a slim parsnip, with flesh which is white and hard. Hot and pungent, horseradish is usually used grated — finely or coarsely — and added to classic horseradish sauce, pickles and marinades. Its flavour is dimmed by slow cooking.

Juniper Berries

These grow on bushes or small trees related to the conifer family and native to Europe. The tiny cones the bushes bear turn into bluish-black juniper berries which are available fresh or dried. Used in the distillation of some types of gin, the berries are much appreciated in Scandinavian and German cuisine and are especially good in pickles, stews and braises of game. The berries were mentioned in the Bible and considered a symbol of personal protection against evil spirits and wild animals.

Marjoram

Native to Western Asia and the Mediterranean, marjoram is closely related to oregano and the mint family and is associated with love and romance. The herb grows extensively in France, Portugal and the Balkans and has grey-green leaves and a pleasingly aromatic flavour with a hint of mint. It is excellent with lamb, Italian tomato dishes, salads, green beans, kidney beans and chicken.

Mint

An ancient herb, all mints are the leaves of perennial plants native to Western Asia and the Mediterranean but grown and used worldwide. Its green leaves are strong, sweetish and unmistakable in flavour. Mint adds a fillip to summer fruit cups and is also the basis of mint sauce and jelly, traditionally served in Britain with lamb. Additionally, it is tossed with new potatoes and peas, and used for garnishing.

Mixed Herbs

This is a blend of assorted dried or fresh herbs and very much an all-purpose flavouring. When dried, the mixture usually comprises basil, oregano, marjoram and thyme but can also be made from parsley, chives, chervil, savory, oregano or marjoram and basil.

Mustard

Native to Europe and Asia, mustard is related to the cabbage family and was used in prehistoric times. Now cultivated in North America, East Africa, Northern Europe and Britain, mustard is an annual plant yielding hot-tasting seeds. The two types most widely used are the black or brown and white or creamy yellow. Mustard has a mildish taste but is naturally fiery. Legend has it that the name mustard is a corruption of mustseeds, as the seeds were marinated in must or grape juice during the Roman occupation of Britain.

Oregano

Native to ancient Rome and introduced to Britain at the time of the Roman occupation, oregano is a very pungent, slightly peppery and characterful herb, green-leafed, which grows steadfastly all over Europe. Its flavour makes it a natural addition to strong-flavoured Italian, Spanish and Mexican dishes (it is also grown in Mexico) and its other name is wild marjoram.

Parsley

One of the most commonly used herbs of all, and popular in mediaeval times, parsley was originally native to the Mediterranean but now grows abundantly everywhere, affording flavouring to all manner of savoury dishes. Parsley can be smooth, curly or frond-like and is generally an emerald green colour, more handsome fresh than dried. It is used worldwide as a garnish.

Rosemary

"Rosemary for remembrance" was mentioned by Ophelia in Hamlet and many other legends are attached to this classic herb, native to the Mediterranean but now growing profusely all over Europe. The leaves, from an evergreen shrub of the mint family, are grey-green and resemble thick, curved and 1 inch (2.5cm) long needles. Sweetly aromatic and fragrant, the herb is well-recommended for adding to lamb but also goes well with pork, and adds an unusual taste to braises and stews of chicken and veal.

Sage

Another herb native to Europe, sage was used by the ancient Romans and Greeks while the Arabs were sure it guaranteed long life. Also a member of the mint family, sage grows happily in all temperate countries of the world and its soft green leaves are especially sympathetic towards pork and bacon.

Savory

Native to Southern Europe but now growing worldwide, savory is yet another member of the mint family but is a more subtle and gentle herb than its relatives and its small green leaves are reminiscent of a mild version of thyme. Unless home-grown, savory is available only dried and ground.

Sorrel

Native to Europe and the Middle East, sorrel was introduced into Britain in the latter part of the 16th century by the French. It is a member of the dock family and its large green leaves can be used as a substitute for spinach, in French sorrel soup and in salads. It has a slightly acid flavour and is much loved in the Soviet Union.

Tansy

Known to the ancient Greeks and Romans, tansy has very attractive lacy leaves, fern-like in appearance and deep green. It makes a simple but unusual decoration though is rarely used for culinary purposes due to its peculiar flavour. It bears charming bright yellow flowers which can be cut and used for decoration. In Victorian times, some custards, puddings and cakes were flavoured with chopped tansy, a custom which has long since faded.

Tarragon

A herb native to Siberia and Asia, tarragon moved to South Europe and France about the time of the Middle Ages. The flavour of tarragon is spectacular and lies somewhere between mint and aniseed. One of the essentials of a Bearnaise sauce, tarragon leaves are slim and deep green and make excellent additions to salad dressings, fish stock, Tartare sauce, vinegar, shell fish dishes and omelettes.

Thyme

Native to Southern Europe, thyme grows abundantly in its countries of origin. Related to mint, thyme leaves are greenish-brown and small and its sweet and slightly pungent scent is particularly good in tomato dishes, stuffings for poultry, fish soups and white sauce.

Spices

Allspice

Tasting of three spices — clove, nutmeg and cinnamon — allspice comes from Central and South America and the West Indies, the only spice grown in the Western hemisphere. It is the round, pea-sized fruit of an evergreen tree belonging to the myrtle family and is very widely used in North America. When whole, allspice can be added to pickles, chutneys, beef stews, casseroles and pot roasts. When ground, it can be added to apple dishes, gingerbreads, other spice cakes and milk puddings. It is interesting when lightly sprinkled over hot coffee or chocolate.

Anise Seed

Also known as aniseed and a native of Eastern Mediterranean countries, this liquorice-flavoured spice was mentioned in the Bible and the Romans kept anise plants near their pillows to prevent bad dreams. The seed is small and oval, not unlike caraway, and is well-loved by Italians who use it in cakes and fancy breads. Oil of anise is used to flavour confectionery, liqueurs and cough medicines.

Cardamom

Cardamom is the expensive seed pod of the dried fruit of a plant belonging to the ginger family. The pod is creamy in colour and, once opened, reveals tiny black seeds which contain all the bitter-sweet, aromatic and slightly lemony flavour which characterize this spice. Very much used in Indian cooking — it is one of the spices combined in a traditional curry powder — cardamom is Scandinavia's most popular flavouring and finds its way into Danish pastries, yeast cakes, sweetbreads and biscuits. Its heady flavour complements that of coffee very well.

Cayenne Pepper (Chilli Pepper)

A fiery red pepper ground from capsicums grown in North and Central America, West Africa and Japan. It should be used with an element of caution.

Chilli Powder or Seasoning

Mild or hot, this is a blend of spices designed for Mexican style food, although it can also be used to season other dishes with equal success. It is made from a base of chilli pepper to which are added garlic, cumin, salt and oregano. It is comparatively mild.

Cinnamon

The world's most important spice, cinnamon is native to the Far East and is made from the dried bark of an evergreen tree belonging to the laurel family. Cinnamon sticks are the quills of rolled bark, otherwise the spice is ground and used as a major flavouring in sweet and savoury dishes. It is a warm brown, aromatic and attractively pungent.

Cloves

Native to the Moluccas Islands (the Spice Islands), cloves are now to be found off the East African coast and resemble a nail in shape, hence their French name of clou. A clove is the dried, unopened bud of an evergreen tree and has a very spikey, pungent flavour and aroma. It is highly acceptable in pickles, chutneys, marinades, hot punches, fish and meat stocks, bread sauce and for 'nailing' into whole hams, oranges for pomanders and whole onions for flavouring. When ground, cloves can be used, sparingly, for spicing baked goods such as puddings, pies and biscuits.

Coriander (Dried)

This is the ripe and dried fruit of a herb belonging to the parsley family and is native to the same countries as fresh coriander. The seeds of the plant are small and vary in colour from creamy white to dark yellow. The flavour is something like a mixture of lemon and sage, and the seeds are frequently used whole for pickling. When ground, they are one of the ingredients of curry powder, and also used to flavour cakes, biscuits and teabreads.

Cumin (Cummin)

Cumin (pronounced come in) is native to the Middle East and India and is a spice which was known before Biblical times and much appreciated by the ancient Egyptians. It is the small dried fruit of an annual plant related to the parsley family and imported from the Middle East, North Africa and Southern Italy. An essential of curry and chilli powder, cumin is also added to Swiss, Dutch and German cheeses and can be used either in seed or ground form. It has a fairly strong, firm taste, spicy, pungent and unique. It is much used in Oriental and Mexican cooking and also finds its way into sauerkraut.

Curry Leaves

Green curry leaves grow on trees native to Asia and add a distinctive flavour to curries and other similar dishes. Readily available in the Orient where they are used fresh, curry leaves imported into the West are usually dried. They can be ground down to a powder in a blender and used in egg dishes, stews, marinades, bastes and rice mixtures. They may also be crumbled between the fingers.

Fennel Seeds

Imported from the Balkans and India, fennel seeds are a member of the parsley family and native to Europe. They are yellow-brown in colour and taste faintly of aniseed. Used whole or ground, fennel is popular in Italy for baked goods and the seeds given an admirable taste to seafood, pickles and poultry dishes.

Fenugreek

Native to Southern Europe, fenugreek is an annual herb and a member of the pea family. It is cultivated in India, the Middle East and South America and is one of the traditional herbs added to a typical curry powder. The seeds are dark yellow, oval and short and the flavour resembles caramel or a hint of burnt sugar. Fenugreek seeds can be used whole or ground in salads, chutneys, pickles and meat stews.

Five Spice Powder (Chinese Five Spice)

A Chinese spice mix consisting of ground star anise, cinnamon, cloves, fennel seed and ginger. It smells of liquorice and is widely used in Chinese cooking. It may also be used in baked goods, pies, marinades, bastes, poultry dishes and rice salads.

Garlic Granules

Dried and coarsely pulverised dried powder made from garlic.

Garam Masala

Indian mixed spice which can vary as much as our own. It can contain roasted and ground coriander, chilli powder, pepper, cinnamon, nutmeg and cloves. It is often used as a basis for curry dishes but generally other spices are added alongside.

Ginger

Native to Southern Asia, ginger is cultivated in the West Indies, South India, Africa and Australia. It is the root of a tuberous and perennial plant akin to the lily and is used very much in both Oriental and Western cooking. Fresh ginger, also called green or root ginger, is sold widely in the UK and, when peeled and crushed or grated, adds a marvellously subtle taste to food. Sun-dried ginger is produced from year-old plants and is a light creamy-beige spice with a distinct and pungent flavour, warming, slightly peppery and penetrating. It has many uses in pickling and baking and is often added to curry powder. Ginger preserved in syrup, as well as crystallized ginger, are produced from fresh green roots or rhizomes which have been previously cleaned.

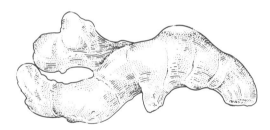

Mace

Mace is the lacy mesh outer covering of the nutmeg and is native to the Moluccas Islands (Spice Islands). It is vivid red while on the tree but turns a golden orange colour when dried. It is an expensive spice, tastes of nutmeg, is quite potent and a little goes a long way. Blades of mace (pieces) are used to flavour drinks, pickles, marinades and some puddings. When ground, mace can be used to flavour baked goods, fish and poultry dishes and chocolate desserts.

Nutmeg

Also native to the Moluccas Islands (Spice Islands), nutmeg is the seed of a peach-like fruit which grows on tall, evergreen trees with leaves like rhododendrons. In colour and appearance, whole nutmeg resembles a miniature walnut. Nutmeg is generally grated and used to scent baked goods, milk puddings, marinades and some sauces. It has an unmistakable and unique flavour, exotic and pungent and should be used sparingly.

Paprika

Native to Central America, paprika is a bright orangey-red pepper made from sweet red peppers (capsicums) growing abundantly in Hungary and Spain. It is dried and ground then used as a flavouring agent and garnish. Hungarian paprika, although mild, has marginally more bite to it than other varieties.

Pepper

Native to the Far East, pepper is now exported from the Far East and Latin America. History tells us that pepper was known as early as 3000 BC and was used to preserve and season meat mixtures. It is the world's most favoured spice and is the small dried berry of a perennial climbing plant similar to a vine. It is available black or white and has a distinctive heat to its make-up.

Poppy Seeds

Native to Asia, poppy seeds were known to the ancient Egyptians as long ago as 1500 BC. Cultivated in the Netherlands, Poland, Turkey, Rumania, the Middle East and South America, the seeds come from vivid red poppies and are grey-black in colour with a tempting, nut-like crunch. They are used widely in baking internationally and contain no narcotic properties.

Poultry Seasoning

A blend of spices designed for poultry. The mix depends on the manufacturer but some combinations might be thyme, savory, marjoram and sage.

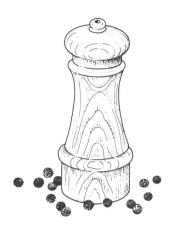

Star Anise

Star anise is the star-shaped dried fruit of a small evergreen tree native to China and related to the magnolia family. It resembles aniseed in flavour and is used not only in Chinese cooking but also to scent liqueurs.

Tandoori Spice Mix

A blend of orange spices used to flavour North Indian and Pakistani roasts and grills which, in their countries of origin, are cooked in a clay oven or tandoor. The spices vary but can include turmeric, chilli powder, cardamom, paprika, garlic granules, cumin, coriander, ground black peppercorns, cinnamon, ginger and nutmeg.

Turmeric

Native to Indonesia and China, most of our turmeric comes from India, the West Indies and South America. It is made from the aromatic roots of a plant belonging to the ginger family and is vivid yellow with a mild taste. It is frequently used in place of saffron to add colour and flavour. It is the basis of Piccalilli.

Saffron

The world's most expensive spice, saffron is native to the Orient and introduced to Spain by the Arabs. It is made from the dried stamens of the cultivated crocus and is golden-orange in colour. It has a most subtle aroma and taste, exotic yet mild. Saffron is much used in Spanish, Balkan and Jewish cooking and was said to have grown in King Solomon's garden. It not only flavours food but also tints it yellow.

Sesame Seed

Native to Asia, sesame seeds are cultivated in India, the Far East, North and Central America and the Balkans. Sesame grows on an herbaceous annual plant to a height of about two feet (60cm) and the seeds, preceded by a colourful blossom, are found in the dark grey hulls. They are pearly-cream, delicate-flavoured and valued for their bland oil. The seeds are used in baked goods when they take on a distinctive nutty taste and texture.

SOUPS AND STARTERS

Giblet Cream Soup

Serves 8

A rich-tasting, creamy soup based on poultry giblets and vegetables.

1oz (25g) butter or margarine
1 set of giblets, approximately 8oz (225g)
4oz (125g) onions, peeled and chopped
4oz (125g) carrots, peeled and sliced
8oz (225g) blanched tomatoes, skinned and chopped
12oz (350g) potatoes, peeled and diced
1¾ pints (1 litre) water
1 tsp lemon juice
1 level tbsp tarragon
2 level tsps salt
⅛ tsp white pepper
½ pints (275ml) milk
croûtons for sprinkling over the tops

1. Melt butter or margarine in a large pan. Add giblets and vegetables. Fry, covered, for 7 minutes until vegetables are soft and light gold.

2. Add water, lemon juice, tarragon and seasonings. Bring to the boil, reduce heat and cover. Simmer steadily for 1½ hours.

3. Remove giblets from pan and use as desired. Liquidize soup until smooth in blender goblet, doing this in 3 or 4 batches.

4. Return to pan and mix in milk. Re-heat until hot before serving, adjust seasoning to taste and ladle into soup bowls. Sprinkle each with croûtons.

New England Fish Chowder

Serves 6 to 8

A classic soup from North America's eastern seaboard. It is often made with clams, though other fish are used as well.

4oz (125g) back bacon, chopped
4oz (125g) onions, peeled and chopped
1 level tbsp flour
1lb (450g) potatoes, peeled and cut into
  ½" (1.25cm) cubes
1½ pints (850ml) milk
1lb (450g) cod or haddock fillets
½ level tsp salt
¼ level tsp nutmeg
⅛ level tsp white pepper

1. Fry bacon in its own fat with onions until soft, allowing 3 to 4 minutes. Stir in flour and cook a further minute.

2. Add potatoes to pan then gradually stir in milk. Bring to the boil, cover and simmer for 15 minutes.

3. Meanwhile, remove skin and any bones from fish. Cut flesh into 1" (2.5cm) cubes. Add to soup and continue to simmer for a further 10 to 15 minutes or until the fish just begins to flake.

4. Season with salt, nutmeg and pepper. Ladle into bowls and serve very hot.

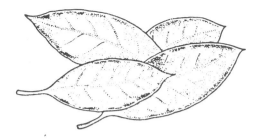

Turkey Soup

Serves 6 to 8

A straight forward soup and a useful way to make the most of a turkey carcass.

1 tbsp salad oil
4oz (125g) onions, peeled and chopped
3oz (75g) carrots, peeled and sliced
3oz (75g) celery, well-scrubbed and sliced
3 pints (1.8 litres) water
a turkey carcass from a 12lb (5.6kg) turkey, broken up
5 juniper berries, coarsely crushed
2 level tsps mixed herbs
1 garlic clove, peeled and crushed
1 small bay leaf
1 2" (5cm) strip of lemon peel
3 level tsps salt
¼ level tsp white pepper

1. Heat oil in a large pan. Add onions, carrots and celery. Fry gently for 10 minutes until soft and very pale brown.

2. Add all remaining ingredients. Bring to the boil, lower heat and cover. Simmer steadily for 1½ hours.

3. Strain into a clean pan, re-heat then serve hot in bowls. Freshly boiled rice may be added to each; so, also, may barley.

Curried Lentil and Carrot Soup

Serves 6 to 8

As orange as a summer sunset, this is an outstanding curried soup which is thickened with breadcrumbs.

1 tbsp salad oil
4oz (125g) onions, peeled and finely chopped
6oz (175g) red split lentils
4oz (125g) carrots, peeled and very thinly sliced
1 level tbsp Madras curry powder
2 pints (1.2 litres) boiling water
1½ level tsp salt
¼ level tsp paprika
crumbs made from 2 slices of wholemeal bread
chopped fresh coriander for sprinkling over the top

1. Heat oil in a large pan. Add onions and fry for about 10 minutes or until light golden.

2. Add lentils and cook for 1 minute, stirring all the time. Mix in carrots and curry powder. Cook for 2 minutes.

3. Add water, salt and paprika. Bring to the boil, lower heat and cover. Simmer for 1 hour, stirring occasionally.

4. Add crumbs to soup and continue to cook for a further 5 to 7 minutes, stirring. Ladle into soup bowls and sprinkle with coriander.

Taj Mahal Soup

Serves 6

More a soup meal than a soup, serve in individual bowls with spoons and forks. Accompany with warm bread.

1½lb (675g) neck of lamb fillet
1½oz (40g) flour, well seasoned with salt and pepper
1oz (25g) butter or margarine
2 tsps salad oil
4oz (125g) onions, peeled and finely chopped
1 garlic clove, peeled and crushed
seeds from 6 opened-out cardamom pods
2 level tbsps tandoori spice mixture
1 level tbsp tomato purée
2 level tbsps chopped fresh coriander
2 rounded tbsps mango chutney
¼ level tsp powdered cloves
¼ level tsp ground ginger
½ level tsp salt
1½ pints (850ml) chicken stock

1. Trim excess fat off meat. Slice into ¼" (6mm) thick rounds and toss in the seasoned flour.

2. Heat butter or margarine and salad oil in a large saucepan. Add meat and fry quickly on both sides until brown. Remove to plate and leave aside temporarily.

3. Add onions, garlic and cardamom seeds to remaining fat in pan. Fry until pale gold.

4. Stir in remaining flour with tandoori spice mixture and cook for 2 minutes, stirring.

5. Add all remaining ingredients and return lamb to pan.

6. Bring to the boil, stirring. Lower heat and cover. Simmer for 1 hour, then cool and pour into a large bowl.

7. Cover and refrigerate overnight. The next day, skim off hard layer of fat that rises to the top. Re-heat before serving until piping hot.

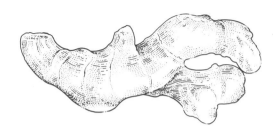

Vegetable Broth

Serves 8

A healthy enough soup, filled with cheerful colours.

1oz (25g) butter or margarine
2oz (50g) carrots, peeled and diced
4oz (125g) onions, peeled and finely chopped
4oz (125g) red pepper, deseeded and cut into fine shreds
4oz (125g) celery, well-scrubbed and thinly sliced
1 can (1lb 14oz or 800g) tomatoes
1¾ pints (1 litre) water
3 level tsps salt
pepper to taste
1 level tsp marjoram

1. Melt butter or margarine in a large saucepan. Add all prepared vegetables, with the exception of tomatoes, and cook, covered, over a low heat for 8 minutes. Stir frequently.

2. Mix in tomatoes, first slightly broken up, their juice, water, salt, pepper and marjoram. Bring to the boil, lower heat and cover. Simmer for 45 minutes.

3. Ladle into soup bowls and serve very hot.

Minestrone Soup

Serves 6 to 8

Follow previous recipe, adding 2oz (50g) broken macaroni to soup 10 minutes before it is ready. Sprinkle tops with grated Parmesan cheese.

Chilled Carrot Vichyssoise

Serves 8 to 9

A top drawer soup for summer pleasure.

1½lb (675g) carrots, peeled and thinly sliced
1½lb (675g) potatoes, peeled and thinly sliced
2½ pints (1.5 litres) water
8oz (225g) onions, peeled and finely chopped
5 level tsps salt
⅛ level tsp pepper
4 tbsps Grand Marnier
¼ pint (150ml) double cream
chopped chives for sprinkling over the top

1. Place carrots, potatoes, water, onions and salt into a large saucepan.
2. Bring to the boil, lower heat and cover. Simmer for about 30 to 40 minutes or until vegetables are tender.
3. Liquidize in blender goblet, in 2 or 3 batches, until very smooth. Pour into bowl and season with pepper.
4. Cover and chill several hours in the refrigerator. Before serving, stir in Grand Marnier and cream. Sprinkle each serving with chopped chives.

Cold Cheese Soufflés

Serves 2

Characterful little soufflés with plenty of flavour.

1oz (25g) butter or margarine
1oz (25g) plain flour
¼ pint (150ml) milk
1 level tsp gelatine, dissolved in 1 tbsp boiling water
2oz (50g) Cheddar cheese, finely grated
2 Grade 3 eggs, separated
½ level tsp prepared English mustard
½ tsp vinegar
½ tsp Worcestershire sauce
¼ level tsp salt
2 level tsps finely chopped parsley

1. Tie a double band of greaseproof paper round 2 individual soufflé dishes so that it protrudes 1″ (2.5cm) above top edges.
2. Melt butter or margarine in a pan. Stir in flour and cook for 2 minutes without browning. Gradually blend in milk. Cook for 2 minutes, stirring continuously.
3. Remove from heat. Stir in melted gelatine, cheese, egg yolks, mustard, vinegar, Worcestershire sauce and salt.
4. Stiffly whisk egg whites and fold into cheese sauce mixture. Pour into soufflé dishes and chill in the refrigerator until set.
5. Before serving, carefully remove bands of greaseproof paper. Gently press chopped parsley round edges.

Guacamole

Serves 12

An old Mexican favourite, this time based on protein-packed tofu or bean curd. Serve as a dip for parties, accompanied by crackers or Tortilla chips.

1 carton (10½oz or 297g) pasteurized silken tofu, drained
2 medium ripe avocados (about 1¼lb or 575g)
2 tbsps lemon juice
1 level tsp salt
1 garlic clove, peeled and halved
2oz (50g) onion, peeled and quartered
4oz (125g) green pepper, deseeded and cut into wide strips
4oz (125g) tomatoes, blanched, skinned, quartered

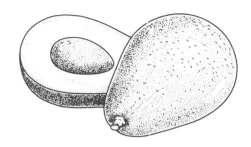

1. Put tofu into blender goblet or food processor.

2. Halve avocados, remove stones and scoop out flesh. Add to tofu with lemon juice, salt and garlic.

3. Run machine until mixture is very smooth. Stop 3 times and wipe down sides of blender goblet or processor bowl with a spatula.

4. Add all remaining ingredients. Continue to run machine until vegetables are well chopped-up.

5. Scrape into a serving bowl and 'bury' one avocado stone into the mixture as it halts browning. Cover and chill lightly before serving.

Camembert Pâté with Brandy

Serves 6 to 8

A slighty heady pâté, and a sophisticated way to end a special meal.

6oz (175g) Camembert cheese
4oz (125g) unsalted butter, softened
3 tsps brandy
½ level tsp tarragon

1. Remove rind from cheese and discard. Place remainder in a blender goblet with butter. Process until very smooth.

2. Add brandy and tarragon. Process again until very well mixed.

3. Spread evenly into a small bowl, cover and refrigerate several hours or until firm. Serve with fingers of hot toast.

Curried Cheese Balls

Makes 30

An ideal taster at any cocktail party.

7oz (200g) soft cream cheese
1½ level tsp mild curry powder
seeds from 6 opened-out cardamom pods
4½ level tbsps sesame seeds, toasted until golden brown

1. Beat cheese until soft. Add curry powder and cardamom seeds. Mix thoroughly.
2. Roll teaspoons of cheese mixture into small balls then coat with sesame seeds.
3. Transfer to a plate covered with greaseproof paper and chill in the refrigerator until firm. Spear onto cocktail sticks before serving.

Tandoori Cheese Balls

Makes 30

A unique snack, also designed for a drinks' party. Their black overcoats are visually intriguing!

Make as curried cheese balls in previous recipe, using the following ingredients.

8oz (225g) soft cream cheese
2 level tsps tandoori spice mixture
1 garlic clove, peeled and crushed
3 to 4 drops tabasco
¼ level tsp salt
pepper to taste
4½ level tbsps dark grey poppy seeds for coating

Fish Roe Pâté

Serves 8 to 11

A smooth, cream-coloured pâté with a certain exclusivity and yet, given that one has a blender or food processor, simplicity itself to make. Also reasonably economical.

8oz (225g) onions, peeled and chopped
1 garlic clove, peeled and crushed
4oz (125g) butter, melted (do not substitute margarine)
1 tbsps lemon juice
1 tbsp light wine vinegar
½ level tsp salt
1½lb (675g) soft fish roes, washed and drained

1. Put all ingredients into a pan. Cover and cook gently for ½ hour, stirring occasionally.
2. Blend, in 2 batches, to a smooth purée in blender goblet or food processor.
3. Spread evenly into a dish, cover with clingfilm and refrigerate several hours until firm. To serve, spoon out onto plates and eat with hot toast.

Italian Gorgonzola Pâté

Serves 6 to 8

A perfect ending to an Italian meal.

6oz (175g) Gorgonzola cheese
4oz (125g) unsalted butter, softened
3 tbsps Marsala
2 level tsps finely chopped chives
⅛ level tsp nutmeg

1. Derind cheese then place in blender with butter. Process until very smooth.

2. Add Marsala, chives and nutmeg. Process again until thoroughly and smoothly mixed.

3. Spoon into a small bowl, cover and refrigerate until firm. Serve with small plain biscuits.

Stuffed Italian Tomatoes

Serves 6

Sometimes Italian plum tomatoes, elongated rather than round, appear in the shops. When they do, make this vegetarian starter for any occasion.

6 plum tomatoes, weighing about 1¼lb or 575g
2oz (50g) fresh white breadcrumbs
2oz (50g) Gruyère cheese, grated
1 rounded tbsp chopped parsley
½oz (15g) trimmed spring onions, finely chopped
1 level tsp basil
¼ level tsp salt
⅛ level tsp pepper
1oz (25g) butter or margarine, melted
2 level tbsps chopped fresh dill for sprinkling over the top

1. Preheat oven to 200°C (400°F), gas mark 6. Grease a 12″ × 8″ (30 × 20cm) shallow, heatproof dish.

2. Wash and dry tomatoes. Halve lengthwise and scoop out pulp directly into a bowl. Reserve tomato shells.

3. Mix pulp with breadcrumbs, cheese, parsley, onions, basil and seasonings. Bind together with melted butter or margarine.

4. Spoon equal amounts into tomato halves then transfer to prepared dish. Cover with lid or foil and bake for 20 minutes. Uncover and continue to cook a further 10 minutes.

5. Shower with chopped dill and serve hot.

Cheese and Onion Dip

Serves 6 to 8

An uncomplicated dip for party occasions, superb with short lengths of celery.

5oz (150g) low fat soft cheese
3 Grade 3 hard-boiled eggs, shelled and cut into eighths
2oz (50g) onion, peeled and grated
½ level tsp powder mustard
1 level tsp tomato purée
½ level tsp salt
⅛ level tsp nutmeg
black pepper
pinch of cayenne pepper

1. Place all ingredients into a blender goblet and process until very smooth.

2. Spread evenly into a small dish. Cover and refrigerate until firm. Serve with brown toast.

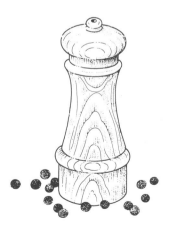

Chicken Liver Pâté

Serves 4

An exquisite, delicate pâté using economically-priced chicken livers.

8oz (225g) chicken livers, washed, dried, coarsely chopped
¼ pint (150ml) single cream
1 level tbsp tomato purée
2 level tsps prepared English mustard
2 tsps Worcestershire sauce
1 level tsp mixed herbs
2 tsps brandy
½ level tsp salt
pinch of black pepper

1. Place all ingredients into a frying pan, bring to the boil and simmer for 5 minutes or until livers are just cooked but still pink inside. Stir once or twice.

2. Remove from heat. Spoon contents of pan into blender goblet or food processor and run machine until mixture is absolutely smooth.

3. Spread evenly into 4 small dishes (such as ramekins). Cover and refrigerate until firm. Eat with crusty French bread or brown rolls.

FISH

Shrimps in Fire Batter

Serves 16

Party fritters which are at their best served freshly cooked and piping hot. They go down well at drinks' parties.

2oz (50g) plain flour
⅛ level tsp salt
⅛ level tsp ground coriander
⅛ level tsp paprika
⅛ level tsp 5-spice powder
seeds from 4 opened-out cardamom pods
1 garlic clove, peeled and crushed
4 tbsps lukewarm water
2 tsps butter or margarine, melted
1 Grade 3 egg white
1 can (7oz or 198g) shrimps, drained and coarsely chopped
oil for deep fat frying

1. Sift flour, salt, coriander, paprika and 5-spice powder into a bowl. Stir in cardamom seeds and crushed garlic.
2. Mix to a smooth batter with water and the butter or margarine. Stiffly whisk egg white and fold into batter. Stir in chopped shrimps.
3. Heat oil until hot and fry rounded teaspoons of mixture for 2 to 3 minutes until puffy and golden.
4. Drain on absorbent kitchen paper, spear with cocktail sticks and serve straight away.

Coley and Rice Hash

Serves 4 to 6

A successful midweek dish, not very beautiful but warming when there's a nip in the air!

4 pints (2.25 litres) water
1½ level tsps salt
8oz (225g) brown rice, washed
6oz (175g) onions, finely chopped
1lb (450g) coley fillet, skinned and cut into
  1" (2.5cm) cubes
1 oz (25g) butter or margarine
½ level tsp marjoram
pepper to taste
4 level tbsps finely chopped parsley

1. Bring water to the boil, add salt, rice and onions. Stir round, cover and simmer for 45 minutes. Drain and return to saucepan.
2. Stir in coley, butter or margarine, marjoram and pepper. Return to boil and simmer for a further 7 minutes or until fish begins to flake.
3. Remove from heat, spoon out onto warm plates and sprinkle thickly with parsley.

Opposite: Vermicelli with Curry Sauce (page 63).

Overleaf: Herb Butters (page 88).

Ceviche

Serves 8

Mexican and quite something to have a fish dish which actually cooks without heat in its own marinade. Fresh lime is one of the essentials.

1½lb (675g) haddock fillets
3 tbsps medium sherry
2 tbsps salad oil
juice of 2 medium lemons
juice of 1 lime
¼ level tsp cayenne pepper
1 garlic clove, peeled and crushed
3oz (75g) onions, peeled and each cut into 8 wedges
2 level tbsps chopped parsley
½ level tsp salt
8oz (225g) crisp lettuce

1. Remove skin and any bones from the fish. Cut flesh into 1″ (2.5cm) cubes and transfer to a dish.

2. Whisk together sherry, oil, lemon and lime juices, cayenne pepper and garlic. Add to fish and toss over and over until well-coated.

3. Dot here and there with pieces of onion then sprinkle with parsley and salt. Cover and leave to marinate in the refrigerator for 8 to 12 hours, turning 3 or 4 times.

4. Before serving, chop lettuce and use to cover 8 plates. Remove onions from fish and discard. Using a slotted spoon, lift out fish cubes and place equal amounts onto lettuce-lined plates.

Lancashire Cod Pie

Serves 6

A fish pie with a distinctive flavour.

1lb (450g) cod fillet
water
1 level tsp salt
1 tbsp salad oil
8oz (225g) onions, peeled and finely chopped
1lb (450g) potatoes, peeled and freshly boiled
1oz (25g) butter or margarine
2 tbsps milk
1 level tsp salt
pepper to taste
3 level tbsps finely chopped parsley
4oz (125g) breadcrumbs
4oz (125g) Lancashire cheese, grated

1. Place cod in a pan with water to cover then sprinkle with salt. Simmer for 10 minutes. Drain, remove skin and bones then flake flesh fairly finely.

2. Heat oil in separate pan. Add onions and fry gently until brown.

3. Drain potatoes and mash finely. Beat in butter or margarine, milk, seasonings and the parsley. Stir in flaked fish and onions. Return to saucepan, half cover and heat through slowly until very hot. Stir occasionally.

4. Preheat grill. Spoon hot fish mixture evenly into a 9½″ (24cm) greased, heatproof dish. Combine breadcrumbs and cheese. Sprinkle over surface and brown under a hot grill.

Poached Skate Wings in Brown Butter and Caper Sauce

Serves 6

A well-loved classic, extra good served with boiled potatoes and a selection of cooked seasonal vegetables.

4 halved skate wings, each half approximately 8oz (225g)
1 pint (575ml) water
1 tbsp lemon juice
1 bouquet garni bag
1 bay leaf
a 3" (7.5cm) strip of lemon peel
1 level tsp salt
pepper

Sauce
4oz (125g) butter
4 level tbsps chopped parsley
2 tbsps lemon juice
1 level tbsp drained and chopped capers

1. Wash skate wings and remove any skin. Place in a large frying pan with remaining ingredients.

2. Bring to the boil, cover and simmer for 15 minutes. Drain and keep warm while making sauce.

3. Heat butter fairly slowly and carefully until it turns a deep golden brown. Allow to cool slightly.

4. Mix in remaining ingredients and pour over skate.

Stir-Fry Plaice

Serves 4

Elegantly appealing for those who enjoy a blend of eastern flavours.

1 tbsp salad oil
6oz (175g) onions, peeled and finely chopped
1 garlic clove, peeled and crushed
½oz (15g) fresh ginger, peeled and crushed
  (use a garlic press)
12oz (350g) plaice fillets, cut into 1" (2.5cm) strips
8oz (225g) unpeeled courgettes, washed, dried, cut into
  matchstick-sized strips
2oz (50g) celery, well-scrubbed and cut as courgettes
1 level tbsp cornflour
¼ pint (150ml) fish stock or water
2 tsps soy sauce
1 tsp Worcestershire sauce
½ level tsp salt
pepper to taste

1. Heat oil in a pan, add onions, garlic and ginger. Fry for 2 to 3 minutes, stirring.

2. Stir in plaice, courgettes and celery then, using 2 spoons, stir-fry for a further 4 minutes.

3. Blend cornflour with 2 tablespoons of cold fish stock or water. Stir into pan with remaining stock or water, soy and Worcestershire sauces and seasonings.

4. Bring to the boil, cover and simmer for 5 to 6 minutes. Serve with vermicelli.

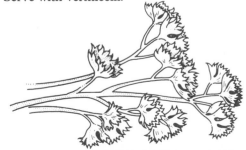

Salmon Stuffed Potatoes — Indian Style

Serves 6

A surprise package all round!

6 baking potatoes, each 8oz (225g)
1oz (25g) butter or margarine
1oz (25g) desiccated coconut
1 level tbsp Madras curry powder
1 level tsp turmeric
1 can (7oz or 198g) pink salmon, drained and flaked
1 level tsp onion salt
pepper to taste
3oz (75g) Cheddar cheese, grated

1. Lightly grease a baking tray. Preheat oven to 190°C (375°F), gas mark 5.

2. Wash, scrub and dry potatoes. Prick well with a fork and stand on baking tray. Bake in oven centre for 1½ to 2 hours or until tender.

3. Melt butter or margarine in a pan. Add coconut, curry powder and turmeric. Cook for 5 minutes.

4. Place curry mixture in a bowl with flaked salmon, onion salt and pepper. Halve jacket potatoes and remove insides, leaving skins whole. Mash coarsely and stir into the salmon mixture.

5. Pile filling back into shells. Sprinkle with grated cheese and return to oven. Bake for 20 to 25 minutes then flash under a hot grill to brown.

Tuna Meringue Pie

Serves 4

A delicious pasta pie which is uncomplicated to make and reasonably priced.

4oz (125g) pasta shells
boiling salted water
1 can (7oz or 198g) tuna, drained and flaked
5 tbsps single cream
½ level tsp salt
¼ level tsp oregano
pepper to taste
2 Grade 3 eggs, separated
3oz (75g) Gruyère cheese, grated

1. Butter an 8½" (22cm) square, shallow, ovenproof dish. Preheat oven to 200°C (400°F), gas mark 6.

2. Cook pasta in plenty of boiling salted water for 10 minutes or until just tender. Drain thoroughly.

3. Combine pasta with tuna, cream, salt, oregano, pepper and egg yolks. Spoon evenly into dish.

4. Stiffly whisk egg whites. Spread over fish mixture then sprinkle with cheese.

5. Bake towards top of oven for 15 minutes until cheese has melted and is golden.

Fresh Halibut Quenelles

Serves 4 to 6

High in the luxury stakes, these are delicate poached fish cakes coated with a highly unusual cream sauce.

½ pint (275ml) water
4oz (125g) butter or block margarine
5oz (150g) plain flour ⎫
¼ level tsp salt ⎬ *sifted together*
4 Grade 3 eggs, well-beaten
1¼lb (575g) skinned and boned halibut, cubed
¼ level tsp tarragon
extra water for cooking
¼ level tsp salt
5 drops of tabasco sauce

1. Put water into a saucepan then add butter or margarine. Melt over a low heat and bring to the boil. Stir in sifted flour and salt in one go. Beat hard until mixture forms a ball in centre of pan, leaving sides clean. Cool for 5 minutes.

2. Gradually beat in eggs until paste is smooth and glossy and forms soft peaks.

3. Purée raw fish in blender or food processor. Add paste from saucepan with tarragon and seasonings. Purée again until smooth. Transfer to bowl then cover securely and chill overnight.

4. Before serving, fill a frying pan with water and bring to the boil. Scoop out the fish mixture with a large tablespoon, packing it down tightly into bowl of spoon. Gently slide into simmering water and poach for 15 minutes.

5. Lift Quenelles onto a plate lined with a damp tea towel. Serve immediately with the sauce below.

Watercress Quenelle Sauce

1½oz (40g) butter or block margarine
1½oz (40g) flour
½ pint (275ml) milk
1 carton (5oz or 142ml) soured cream
juice of ½ small lemon
juice of ½ small orange
2 level tbsps very finely chopped watercress
½ level tsp salt
2 Grade 2 eggs, separated

1. Melt butter or margarine in a pan. Add flour and cook for 1 minute.

2. Gradually blend in milk, cream and fruit juices. Cook, stirring all the time, until sauce comes to the boil and thickens. Simmer for 2 minutes and leave over minimal heat.

3. Quickly stir in watercress, salt and egg yolks. Whisk egg whites to a stiff snow then beat about one-third into sauce.

4. Gently fold in remaining egg white with large metal spoon. Serve over the halibut Quenelles.

Monkfish Cocktail Salads

Serves 4

Based on the highly regarded Waldorf salad, this makes a super autumn or winter meal starter.

1lb (450g) monkfish, boned, skinned, cut into
  ½" (1.25cm) cubes
½ pint (275ml) water
1 tsp lemon juice
½ level tsp salt
8oz (225g) peeled prawns
5oz (150g) dessert apples, cored, cut into ¼" (6mm)
  cubes, tossed in 1 tsp lemon juice
4oz (125g) celery, well-scrubbed and thinly sliced
2oz (50g) walnuts, coarsely chopped
4 round tbsps mayonnaise
4 rounded tbsps double cream
¼ level tsp salt
⅛ level tsp paprika

1. Place monkfish in a pan with water to cover. Add 1 teaspoon lemon juice and salt. Bring to the boil, cover and simmer for 8 minutes. Drain and cool.

2. Mix together the monkfish, prawns, apples, celery and walnuts.

3. Whisk together mayonnaise, cream, salt and paprika. Add to fish mixture and toss over and over until well-coated.

4. Divide between 6 glasses and serve at room temperature.

Savoury Crumbed Skate

Serves 4

A dish for all those who value the full flavour of fresh skate.

½oz (40g) plain flour
½ level tsp salt
¼ level tsp paprika
4 halved skate wings, each half approximately 8 oz (225g)
1 Grade 2 egg } *beaten together*
1 tbsp milk
2oz (50g) Weetabix, finely crushed
4 tbsps salad oil

1. Preheat oven to 190°C (375°F), gas mark 5. Mix together flour and seasonings.

2. Wash and dry skate. Coat with seasoned flour then dip in egg and milk mixture. Cover well with Weetabix crumbs and leave about 30 minutes for coating to settle.

3. Pour oil into a large baking dish and heat in the oven for 5 minutes. Arrange skate in dish and cook just above oven centre for 25 to 30 minutes until golden.

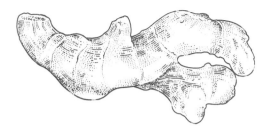

Shrimps in Ginger and Lime Sauce

Serves 4

A starter cocktail with a magical aroma and taste. Accompany with brown bread and butter.

6 level tbsps mayonnaise
finely grated peel of 1 lime
1 tsp lime juice
½oz (15g) fresh ginger, peeled and finely grated
⅛ level tsp salt
⅛ level tsp paprika
1 can (7oz or 198g) shrimps, drained
1 medium avocado, peeled, stone removed, flesh cut into
   ¼" (6mm) cubes
¼ of a large melon, flesh cut into ½" (1.25cm) cubes
4 heaped tsps finely chopped parsley

1. Beat together mayonnaise, lime peel and juice, grated ginger, salt and paprika.

2. Stir in the shrimps and diced avocado.

3. Divide melon between 4 glasses. Spoon shrimp mixture over top and sprinkle each with 1 teaspoon of chopped parsley.

Fisherman's Stew

Serves 4 to 5

Different from the usual run-of-the-mill fish dishes, this one is for all the family to share and enjoy.

1½lb (675g) potatoes, peeled and sliced
12oz (350g) onions, peeled and thinly sliced
1 pint (575ml) water
¼ pint (150ml) milk
1 level tsp salt
1lb fresh haddock fillet, skinned and cut into
   1" (2.5cm) cubes
3 rounded tbsps chopped fresh dill or parsley

1. Put potatoes, onions, water, milk and salt into a large saucepan. Slowly bring to the boil, lower heat and cover. Simmer for 20 minutes.

2. Add fish and cook a further 10 minutes or until it just begins to flake.

3. Spoon out onto warm plates and sprinkle each with the fresh dill or parsley.

Tuna Patties

Makes 6

These are light and puffy patties which are best enjoyed straight from the oven with a well seasoned white sauce and a selection of seasonal cooked vegetables.

4oz (125g) cottage cheese
4oz (125g) cold butter, grated
4oz (125g) plain flour, sifted
½ level tsp salt
1 can (7oz or 198g) tuna, drained and flaked
1 level tbsp lemon-flavoured mayonnaise
1 level tsp tomato purée
½ level tsp mustard powder
¼ level tsp pepper
1 Grade 4 or 5 egg, beaten
1oz (25g) Cheddar cheese, grated

1. Preheat oven to 220°C (425°F), gas mark 7. Lightly grease a baking tray.

2. Knead together cottage cheese, butter, flour and ¼ teaspoon salt until smooth. Wrap and refrigerate for 30 minutes.

3. Mix tuna with mayonnaise, tomato purée, mustard, remaining salt and pepper to taste. Mix well.

4. Roll out pastry thinly and cut into 12 rounds with a 3½" (9cm) biscuit cutter.

5. Place 6 rounds on prepared tray. Spoon equal amounts of tuna mixture onto each. Brush edges of pastry with egg then place remaining pastry rounds on top. Press edges well together to seal.

6. Make 3 incisions in the top of each pattie. Brush with egg and sprinkle with cheese. Bake towards top of oven for 20 minutes. Serve warm.

Prawn Patties

Makes 6

Make as Tuna Patties but use 6oz (175g) coarsely chopped prawns instead of tuna.

Smoked Haddock Patties

Makes 6

Make as Tuna Patties but use 8oz (225g) cooked and flaked smoked haddock or cod instead of tuna.

POULTRY

Chicken Stroganoff

Serves 4

Why beef when chicken does equally well? Serve the stroganoff with brown rice and a green salad tossed in French dressing.

1lb (450g) chicken breast fillets
3oz (75g) butter or margarine
1 tsp salad oil
2oz (50g) onions, peeled and finely chopped
12oz (350g) mushrooms, washed, dried and thinly sliced
1 carton (5oz or 142ml) soured cream
3 tbsps dry sherry
2 level tsps tomato purée
½ level tsp salt
cayenne pepper to taste

1. Wash and dry chicken breasts. Beat between 2 sheets of greaseproof paper until thin. The best implement to use is a wooden mallet or rolling pin.

2. Cut into ½" (1.25cm) wide strips. Melt butter or margarine in a saucepan. Add oil and onions and fry until soft but not brown.

3. Mix in chicken and cook for 4 minutes. Remove from pan and keep hot.

4. Stir mushrooms into pan and cook for 4 minutes.

5. Replace chicken. Add remaining ingredients and bring just up to boiling point, stirring. Serve straight away.

Duck and Vegetable Risotto

Serves 4

Worth making with just half a roast duck, this is a fine-flavoured risotto which goes excellently with seasonal cooked vegetables or salads.

1oz (25g) butter or margarine
2 tbsps salad oil
6oz (175g) onions, peeled and chopped
4oz (125g) carrots, peeled and grated
4oz (125g) mushrooms, washed and thinly sliced
8oz (225g) easy-cook long grain or risotto rice
8oz (225g) cooked duck meat, cut into small cubes
1 pint (575ml) chicken stock
½ level tsp sage
½ level tsp salt
⅛ level tsp pepper
chopped parsley or fresh dill for sprinkling over the top

1. Heat butter or margarine and oil in a saucepan. Add onions and carrots then fry gently for 10 minutes.

2. Add mushrooms and rice. Fry for a further 2 minutes, stirring. Mix in duck meat, stock, sage, salt and pepper.

3. Bring to the boil, lower heat and cover. Simmer for 20 minutes or until rice grains have absorbed all the moisture and are dry and separate.

4. Fluff up with a fork and spoon onto warm plates. Sprinkle with parsley or dill and serve hot.

Turkey Risotto

Serves 4

Make exactly as above, substituting cooked turkey for duck and adding 4oz (125g) cooked peas 5 minutes before risotto has finished cooking. Sprinkle portions with grated Parmesan cheese.

Spiced Indian Chicken

Serves 4

An oriental style dish, this teams happily with freshly boiled rice and a salad of cut-up tomatoes and thinly sliced onions.

1½lb (675g) chicken thighs, skinned
3 rounded tbsps natural yoghurt
1 tbsp milk
1 level tsp garlic salt
1 level tsp garam masala
1 level tsp powdered ginger
4 dried curry leaves, coarsely crushed
1 level tsp coriander
1 level tsp cumin powder
2 level tsps paprika
1 tbsp salad oil
¼ pint (150ml) boiling water

1. Wash and dry chicken. Beat together all remaining ingredients, except water, in shallow bowl.

2. Add chicken thighs and baste with liquid. Cover and marinate for 8 hours, turning twice.

3. Put into a frying pan, leave uncovered and boil for 5 minutes.

4. Cover and continue to simmer for a further 10 minutes. Pour in water and bubble gently for a further 15 minutes, keeping pan half covered.

Saffron Chicken

Serves 4

Expensively spiced with saffron, what better way of dressing up chicken? Serve with brown rice and chutney.

2lb (900g) chicken joints
6oz (175g) onions, peeled but left whole
12oz (350g) carrots, peeled and thickly sliced
4oz (125g) celery, well-scrubbed and sliced
1 level tsp turmeric
1 level tsp salt
pepper
8 saffron strands
cold water
2oz (50g) butter or margarine
2oz (50g) flour
1 oz (25g) desiccated coconut
½ level tsp salt
paprika

1. Place chicken joints, onions, carrots, celery, turmeric, salt, pepper and saffron strands in a large pan.

2. Cover with water. Bring to the boil, lower heat and cover. Simmer for 45 to 50 minutes.

3. Drain chicken pieces and remove meat from bones. Cut into large cubes and arrange in an 8″ (20cm) square, shallow dish.

4. Strain chicken stock and reserve 1 pint (575ml). Melt butter or margarine in a pan. Stir in flour and cook for 2 to 3 minutes. Gradually blend in reserved stock.

5. Cook, stirring, until sauce comes to the boil and thickens. Mix in coconut and salt then simmer for 3 minutes.

6. Pour over chicken and garnish by sprinkling with paprika.

Coronation Chicken

Serves 6 to 8

Now in the height of fashion, this dish takes a fairly long time to make but is worth the effort. It is a classy party dish for a cold buffet and quantities may be doubled or trebled, depending on numbers.

3½lb (1.6kg) roasting chicken
cold water
2oz (50g) carrots, peeled and sliced
1 bouquet garni bag
1 level tsp salt
6 peppercorns
1 tbsp salad oil
2 oz (50g) onion, peeled and finely chopped
2 level tsps mild curry powder
1 level tsp tomato purée
3fl oz (75ml) dry white wine
2fl oz (50ml) chicken stock
1 bay leaf
½ level tsp castor sugar
¼ level tsp salt
pepper to taste
1 tsp lemon juice
¾ pint (450ml) mayonnaise
3 level tbsps mango chutney, sieved

1. Place chicken in large pan and cover with cold water. Add carrots, bouquet garni bag, salt and peppercorns. Bring to the boil, lower heat and cover. Simmer for 45 minutes or until chicken is cooked.

2. Remove from stock and cool. Heat oil separately in a pan then add onion and curry powder. Fry for 3 to 4 minutes. Stir in tomato purée, wine, stock and bay leaf.

3. Bring to the boil, stirring. Add sugar, salt, pepper and lemon juice. Simmer, uncovered, for 10 minutes. Strain and cool.

4. Gradually beat sauce into mayonnaise then stir in sieved chutney. Remove chicken meat from bones. Cut into 1″ (2.5cm) cubes.

5. Toss chicken in about two-thirds of the sauce and arrange on a bed of rice. Hand round leftover sauce separately.

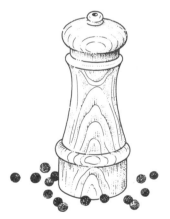

Slimmers' Chinese Chicken

Serves 4

A meal that all the family can share, I suggest slimmers serve their own portion over a bed of hot bean sprouts which is less fattening than rice or pasta.

12oz (350g) chicken breast fillet, minced
4oz (125g) onions, peeled and chopped
1 garlic clove, peeled and crushed
10oz (275g) Chinese leaves, finely shredded
4oz (125g) mushrooms, washed, dried, thinly sliced
1 level tsp 5-star spice
2 level tsps cornflour
2 tbsps light soy sauce
2 tsps chilli sauce
1 tbsp oyster sauce

1. Put minced chicken, onions and garlic into a heavy pan or wok. Dry-fry fairly briskly for 5 minutes, stirring all the time.

2. Add prepared vegetables and continue to stir-fry for a further 7 minutes.

3. Mix in all remaining ingredients and cook a further 4 to 5 minutes, stirring constantly.

Indonesian Turkey Breast Kebabs

Serves 4

Kebabs with a difference, these should be served with bowls of fluffy rice and delicate chutney.

1lb (450g) turkey breast fillets, cut into
½" (1.25cm) cubes
½oz (15g) desiccated coconut, soaked in 4 tbsps boiling water and then strained
4oz (125g) onions, peeled and grated
1 garlic clove, peeled and crushed
2 chillies, seeds removed and finely chopped
2 level tsps ground coriander
2 level tsps light brown soft sugar
½oz (15g) ground almonds
1 tbsp lemon juice
½ level tsp salt

1. Place turkey cubes in a deep bowl. Whisk together all remaining ingredients, pour over turkey and cover. Marinate for 5 to 6 hours, stirring occasionally.

2. Spear turkey onto 4 long skewers and grill until brown and cooked through; about 10 minutes, turning 3 times. Accompany with the sauce below.

Eastern Sauce

1 level tsp castor sugar
1 level tbsp cornflour
¼ pint (150ml) cold water
1 chicken stock cube, crumbled
2 tbsps medium sherry
2 tbsp oyster sauce
1 tbsp light soy sauce
liquid in which turkey was marinated

1. Place all ingredients into a pan. Bring to the boil, stirring.

2. Simmer gently for 1 minute.

Chicken Brawn

Serves 6 to 8

Designed particularly for summer, this is a lightly spiced main course which goes very well with assorted salads.

4lb (1.8kg) chicken
1 pint (575ml) cold water
10oz (275g) onions, peeled
4oz (125g) carrots, peeled and thickly sliced
1 stick of celery, well-scrubbed and broken into 4 pieces
1 garlic clove, peeled and halved
2 sprigs of parsley
1 bouquet garni bag
1 level tsp tarragon
2 level tsps salt
2 packets of gelatine (each 0.4oz or 11g)
juice of ½ medium lemon
3 level tbsps finely chopped parsley

1. Skin chicken and remove fat. Place in a large pan with water, onions, carrots, celery, garlic, parsley sprigs, bouquet garni bag, tarragon and salt.

2. Bring to the boil, lower heat and cover. Simmer for 1 hour. Strain stock and skim off fat. Make up to 1½ pints (850ml) with extra cold water.

3. Add gelatine to ¼ pint (150ml) chicken stock. Pour into saucepan and melt over a low heat, stirring continuously. Combine with remaining stock and refrigerate until just on the point of setting.

4. Remove chicken from carcass. Cut into ½" (1.25cm) cubes and arrange over base of a 10" (25cm) round dish.

5. Sprinkle with lemon juice, coat with gelatine mixture and refrigerate until firmly set. Sprinkle with parsley and spoon portions onto plates. If preferred, the brawn may be set in 6 or 8 individual dishes.

Marinaded Drumsticks

Serves 2

A generous portion for each, these Chinese style drumsticks are best eaten with stir-fry vegetables (packeted or home made) and rice or Chinese noodles.

8 chicken drumsticks, skin removed

Marinade
3 tbsps soy sauce
1 garlic clove, peeled and crushed
2oz (50g) fresh ginger, peeled and crushed in garlic press
2 level tbsps clear honey
2 tbsps dry sherry
2 tbsps peanut oil

1. Wash and dry drumsticks. Beat marinade ingredients well together in shallow dish. Add drumsticks, baste well then leave for 3 to 4 hours, turning twice. Keep covered.

2. To cook, arrange drumsticks in frying pan and coat with marinade.

3. Bring liquid to the boil, reduce heat and half cover the pan. Simmer for 25 to 30 minutes or until drumsticks are cooked through and tender.

MEAT AND OFFAL

Reubens

Serves 4

Giant sandwiches, very North American and immensely filling.

8 large slices of continental brown bread (usually in packets
*   and semi-circular or oblong)*
4 slightly rounded tbsps mayonnaise
½ garlic clove, peeled and crushed
8oz (225g) sauerkraut
8oz (225g) sliced Pastrami or cooked salt beef
6oz (175g) Emmental cheese, thinly sliced
½oz (15g) butter or margarine, melted

1. Preheat oven to 200°C (400°F), gas mark 6.

2. Spread bread with mayonnaise into which garlic has been blended.

3. Rinse and drain the sauerkraut thoroughly. Divide between 4 of the bread slices, spreading it over in an even layer.

4. Top with the Pastrami or salt beef and then the sliced cheese.

5. Press remaining slices of bread on top of filling. Hold in place with cocktail sticks pushed through centre of bread and filling.

6. Brush a shallow baking tray with half the melted butter or margarine. Place sandwiches in the tin then brush with remaining fat.

7. Bake, uncovered, for 30 minutes until bread is crisp and golden and the cheese melted. Serve straight away with salad.

Beef Teriyaki

Serves 6

Japanese in style, all it is is good quality beef marinated in a spicy liquid then threaded onto skewers and grilled. A traditional accompaniment is rice.

2lb (900g) rump steak
4fl oz (125ml) salad oil
3 tbsps medium sherry
2 tbsps soy sauce
½ level tsp ground ginger
½ level tsp garlic powder or granules
⅛ tsp cayenne pepper

1. Cut meat into 1″ (2.5cm) cubes and transfer to a bowl.

2. Whisk together remaining ingredients. Pour over meat and cover. Marinate for a minimum of 6 hours, stirring twice or three times.

3. Preheat grill on full. Thread the meat cubes onto 6 long skewers. Brush with marinade and grill for 5 minutes. Turn and baste again then cook for a further 5 minutes. Serve straight away on a bed of rice.

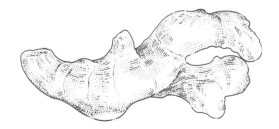

Middle Eastern Aubergines

Serves 4

An attractive dish from desert lands.

2 medium aubergines, about 1½lb or 675g
12oz (350g) neck of lamb fillet, minced
4oz (125g) onions, peeled and minced with the lamb
2 level tbsps tomato purée
1 level tsp marjoram
¼ level tsp salt
4 tbsps water
4 tbsps tomato juice

1. Preheat oven to 180°C (350°F), gas mark 4. Grease a medium-sized roasting tin. Wash and dry aubergines and arrange in tin.

2. Cover with foil and bake in oven centre for 20 minutes. Remove to a chopping board. Increase oven temperature to 220°C (425°F), gas mark 7.

3. Cut stalks off aubergines and discard. Slit each vegetable in half lengthwise and scoop out pulp, leaving ½" (1.25cm) thick shells. Purée pulp in blender or food processor.

4. Fry mince and onions together until brown, allowing 4 to 5 minutes. Stir in aubergine pulp with all remaining ingredients except water and tomato juice. Cover and simmer for 10 minutes.

5. Pack minced filling into aubergine shells and return to clean roasting tin. Add water and tomato juice.

6. Bake near top of oven, uncovered, for 25 minutes. Serve with the Carrot and Lemon Sauce below and accompany with boiled potatoes and cooked green beans.

Carrot and Lemon Sauce

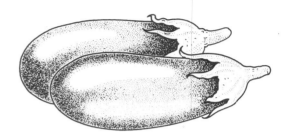

1 1lb 3oz (538g) can carrots, drained and puréed
grated peel of 1 medium lemon
¼ pint (150ml) chicken stock
¼ pint (150ml) water
1 level tsp cornflour
¼ level tsp salt
shake of pepper

1. Put all ingredients into a saucepan.

2. Cover and heat until bubbly, stirring occasionally. Simmer for 4 minutes.

Curried Meat Loaf

Serves 4 to 6

A mildly flavoured, curried loaf, suitable for all the family.

2 tsps salad oil
2 level tsps curry powder
1 level tsp garam masala
4oz (125g) onions, peeled and finely chopped
1lb (450g) lean minced beef
2oz (50g) wholemeal breadcrumbs
1 Grade 3 egg, beaten
½ level tsp salt
pepper to taste

1. Lightly grease a 1lb (450g) loaf tin. Line smoothly with foil then grease again. Preheat oven to 190°C (375°F), gas mark 5.

2. Heat oil in saucepan. Add curry powder, garam masala and onions. Fry over medium heat until golden brown, allowing approximately 7 to 9 minutes.

3. Add fried onion mixture to beef with breadcrumbs, egg and seasonings.

4. Mix thoroughly then spoon into prepared tin. Press down well.

5. Cover with an extra piece of greased foil and bake in oven centre for 45 minutes. Remove foil topping and cook loaf for a further 15 minutes.

6. Invert onto a warm serving plate and cut into thickish slices. Serve with a suitable sauce, chosen from the sauce section. Accompany with boiled potatoes, cooked seasonal vegetables and a dish of mixed pickles.

Braised Steak with Vinegar and Onions

Serves 6

Strong stuff indeed, based on a Belgian traditional recipe. Serve with boiled potatoes and a dish of freshly cooked cabbage or Brussels sprouts.

3lb (1.4kg) stewing beef
¼ pint (150ml) water
12 tbsps vinegar from a jar of pickled onions
1 level tbsp dark brown soft sugar
6 juniper berries, coarsely crushed
½ level tsp tarragon
2 tbsps salad oil
12oz (350g) onions, peeled and finely chopped
12 pickled onions
¼ pint (150ml) water
1 level tsp salt
pepper to taste
4 large slices brown bread with crusts removed
4 level tsp French mustard

1. Cut meat into ½" (1.25cm) cubes. Place in a bowl.

2. Whisk together water, vinegar, sugar, crushed berries and tarragon. Pour over meat and leave to marinate for 8 hours, stirring 3 to 4 times.

3. Heat oil in a large pan. Add chopped onions and fry until golden brown. Stir in drained meat and fry a further 2 to 3 minutes.

4. Mix in the strained marinade, pickled onions, water and seasonings. Bring to the boil, cover and simmer for 1½ hours or until meat is tender.

5. Spread bread with mustard. Stir into stew to thicken then serve piping hot.

China Seas Stir-Fry Pork
Serves 6 to 8

A fine affair, gracious with vermicelli and some light soy sauce as an accompaniment.

1¾lb (800g) pork fillet, washed and dried
2 Grade 2 eggs
1 tbsp light soy sauce
2 tbsps medium sherry
1 garlic clove, peeled and crushed
2 level tbsps cornflour
1 level tsp ground ginger
1 level tsp baking powder
8oz (225g) well-washed celery, thinly sliced
4 tbsps salad oil

1. Chill pork in the refrigerator for 1 hour. Cut into wafer-thin slices.

2. Beat together all remaining ingredients except celery and oil. Put into bowl then add pork. Toss meat over and over to mix.

3. Add celery and toss again. Heat 2 tablespoons of oil in a frying pan or wok. As soon as it sizzles, add one third of the pork and celery mixture.

4. Fry for 5 minutes, turning constantly. Lift out of pan into a warm dish lined with crumpled kitchen paper. Keep warm in a moderate oven.

5. Add another third of mixture to pan. Fry, drain and keep warm as above.

6. Pour rest of oil into pan. Heat until sizzling. Fry last batch of pork mixture as before. Drain and add to dish. Serve straight away.

Tip
To make an easy gravy, bring liquid in pan to a rapid boil with 5 tablespoons hot water. Boil for 1 minute then pour over the pork.

Shaved Lamb with Mixed Vegetables
Serves 2 to 3

An upper crust Irish stew.

12oz (350g) neck of lamb fillet
1lb (450g) potatoes, peeled
boiling water
3 tbsps salad oil
1 garlic clove, peeled and crushed
½oz (15g) fresh ginger, peeled and crushed
  (use garlic press)
8oz (225g) mushrooms, washed, dried, thinly sliced
4oz (125g) green pepper, deseeded and diced
¼ pint (150ml) chicken stock
½ level tsp salt
⅛ level tsp coriander
1 level tbsp tomato purée
1 level tsp cornflour
1 tbsp cold water

1. Chill fillet for 15 minutes in the freezer. Using a very sharp knife, held at an angle of 45°, shave off wafer-thin slices of meat.

2. Cut potatoes into ½" (1.25cm) thick slices. Cook in boiling water for 10 minutes. Drain. Cut into ½" (1.25cm) cubes.

3. Place 2 tablespoons of oil, garlic and ginger into a large frying pan. Cook over a fairly high heat for 2 to 3 minutes. Stir in potatoes, mushrooms and pepper. Continue cooking for a further 2 to 3 minutes.

4. Add remaining tablespoon of oil and the lamb slices. Cook for 3 minutes, stirring all the time. Mix in stock, seasonings and tomato purée. Bring to the boil, cover and simmer for 15 minutes.

5. Blend cornflour with water. Stir into lamb mixture and simmer for 2 minutes. Serve each portion topped with a fried or poached egg.

Piquant Kidneys and Mushrooms

Serves 4 to 6

An exclusive main course for connoisseurs, rich, glorious and comfortable with a big bowl of creamed potatoes sprinkled with either butter-fried flaked almonds or coarsely chopped salted peanuts.

1¼lb (575g) ox kidney
½ pints (275ml) cold milk
12oz (350g) mushrooms, washed, dried, thinly sliced
8 tbsps raspberry vinegar
3 level tsps French mustard
2 level tsps tarragon
2 tbsps salad oil
6 slightly rounded tbsps soured cream
1 level tbsp light brown soft sugar
¼ level tsp salt
1 extra tbsp salad oil
8oz (225g) onions, peeled and chopped
3 level tbsps plain flour

1. Wash and dry kidney. Remove core and cut offal into ½" (1.25cm) cubes. Cover with milk and leave to soak for 1 hour.

2. Place mushrooms in a bowl. Whisk together vinegar, mustard, tarragon, oil, soured cream, sugar and salt. Pour over mushrooms and marinate for 1 hour.

3. Heat oil in a pan. Drain kidneys and fry with the onions for about 5 to 7 minutes or until kidneys are just brown.

4. Stir in flour then cook for a further 2 to 3 minutes. Add mushrooms, with their marinade, then cover and simmer for 45 minutes.

Beef Chow Mein

Serves 6

A western approach to Chinese food but none-the-less commendable with noodles and a dish of freshly cooked Chinese leaves or mange-tout

2lb (900g) rump steak, trimmed of fat
1 tbsp dark soy sauce
1 tsp chilli sauce
1 tbsp Hoi Sin sauce (Chinese barbecue sauce)
1 tbsp medium sherry
1 garlic clove, peeled and crushed
8oz (225g) mushrooms, washed, dried and sliced
4oz (125g) celery, well-scrubbed and thinly sliced
4oz (125g) onion, peeled and cut into very thin slices
4oz (125g) green pepper, deseeded and cut into thin strips
3 level tbsps cornflour
1 can (10oz or 270g) bean sprouts, well-drained
½ pint (275ml) beef stock
1 tbsp oyster sauce

1. Wash and dry meat then cut into thin strips of about 3" × ½" (7.5 × 1.25cm).

2. Beat together the soy, chilli and Hoi Sin sauces, sherry and garlic. Add beef, cover and leave to marinate for 2 hours. Lift meat out with a slotted spoon directly onto a plate.

3. Heat a wok or large and heavy frying pan until hot. Add meat in about 5 or 6 batches, stir-frying each for three-quarter minute before adding the next.

4. Add all the vegetables and stir-fry briskly for a further 3 minutes. Blend in cornflour then add bean sprouts, stock, oyster sauce and marinade liquid in which the meat was standing. Cook for 5 minutes.

Cottage Cheese and Minced Beef Slice

Serves 4

Crisply tender and with an appetizing filling, this makes an inviting meal for lunch or supper.

1 tsp salad oil
1 small garlic clove, peeled and crushed
4oz (125g) lean minced beef
1 level tsp plain flour
1 level tbsp finely chopped parsley
1 level tsp tomato purée
¼ level tsp salt
pepper to taste

Pastry
4oz (125g) cottage cheese
4oz (125g) cold butter, coarsely grated
4oz (125g) plain flour, sifted
¼ level tsp salt
beaten egg for brushing

1. For filling, heat oil in a pan. Add garlic and beef then fry for 4 to 5 minutes until brown, stirring frequently.

2. Mix in flour. Cook for 2 minutes then remove from heat. Add parsley, tomato purée, salt and pepper to taste. Cover and leave to cool.

3. Place cottage cheese, butter, flour and salt into a bowl. Knead all together until smooth then wrap and refrigerate for 30 minutes.

4. Grease a baking tray. Preheat oven to 220°C (425°F), gas mark 7.

5. On a lightly floured surface, roll out pastry into a rectangle measuring 11" × 9" (28 × 23cm).

6. Place meat mixture down one length. Brush pastry edges with beaten egg then fold over pastry and seal by pinching edges well together.

7. Transfer to baking tray then make several slits with a knife on top. Brush with beaten egg and bake just above oven centre for 20 to 25 minutes until golden brown. Cut into slices to serve.

Saté Babi

Serves 4

Indonesian kebabs made from pork. Serve with the Peanut Sauce on page 65 and freshly cooked rice.

1lb (450g) pork tenderloin (fillet)
4oz (125g) onions, peeled and each one quartered
1 garlic clove, peeled and halved
4 level tsps ground coriander
*2 level tsps hot chutney (Indonesian Sambal Manis
   if available)*
1 tbsp soy sauce
1 level tbsp dark brown soft sugar
½ level tsp salt
¼ level tsp white pepper

1. Wash and dry pork then cut into 1" (2.5cm) cubes.

2. Put onions, garlic, coriander and chutney into blender goblet or food processor. Run machine until mixture forms a purée.

3. Spoon into bowl then add soy sauce, sugar, salt and pepper.

4. Add pork cubes and toss over and over in the purée mixture. Cover and leave to marinate for 6 hours, turning twice or three times.

5. Thread onto 4 large skewers and grill under a high heat for 12 to 15 minutes, turning twice and brushing with any remaining marinade. Serve straight away.

Moroccan Lamb

Serves 4 to 6

A beauty from North Africa which should be served with white bread or crisp rolls.

2lb (900g) neck of lamb fillet, fat-trimmed
12 saffron strands
½ level tsp cinnamon
½ level tsp ground ginger
½ pint (275ml) chicken stock, well-seasoned
3 level tbsps clear honey
2 tbsps salad oil
1lb (450g) shallots, peeled
1 level tsp salt

1. Cut lamb into 1″ (2.5cm) medallions. Put into pan with saffron, cinnamon, ginger, stock and 2 tablespoons of honey.

2. Bring to the boil, lower heat and half cover. Simmer gently for 30 minutes.

3. Meanwhile, heat remaining honey and salad oil in a large frying pan. When hot and sizzling, add shallots and fry gently until deep golden brown. Turn fairly frequently.

4. Add to lamb with any left-over liquid. Season with salt, half cover and continue to simmer for a further 20 to 30 minutes or until lamb and shallots are tender and most of the juices have evaporated.

Crumbled Kidneys

Makes 16

Cocktail bites with a touch of originality, though simple to make.

8oz (225g) lambs' kidneys
2 level tbsps flour, well-seasoned with salt and pepper
1 Grade 3 egg, beaten
2oz (50g) fresh white breadcrumbs ⎫
1 level tsp powder mustard ⎬ *mixed together*
1 level tsp mixed herbs ⎭
1oz (25g) butter or margarine
1 tsp salad oil
1 garlic clove, peeled and crushed

1. Wash kidneys and halve lengthwise, remove cores and skin. Cut each kidney into quarters.

2. Coat with flour, roll in egg then toss in breadcrumb mixture.

3. Heat butter or margarine and oil in a pan until hot. Stir in garlic and cook for 1½ minutes.

4. Add kidneys and fry for 10 to 12 minutes until golden brown and crisp.

5. Drain on crumpled kitchen paper then thread a cocktail stick through each. Serve hot.

Lambs' Liver Casserole

Serves 4 to 6

A sound family meal for middle of the week eating.

1½lb (675g) lambs' liver
4 level tbsps flour, well-seasoned with salt and pepper
2oz (50g) margarine
4oz (125g) onions, peeled and finely chopped
4oz (125g) celery, well-scrubbed and thinly sliced
¼ pint (150ml) chicken stock
1 level tbsps tomato purée
1 level tbsp chopped parsley
½ level tsp salt
pepper to taste
1lb (450g) potatoes, peeled and thinly sliced
boiling salted water
3oz (75g) red Cheshire cheese, grated

1. Grease a 9″ (23cm) square, shallow, ovenproof dish. Preheat oven to 190°C (375°F), gas mark 5.

2. Wash and dry liver then cut diagonally into ¾″ (2cm) strips. Coat with seasoned flour.

3. Heat half the margarine in a pan. Add onions and celery then fry for 2 to 3 minutes. Using a slotted spoon, remove vegetables to a plate lined with absorbent paper.

4. Add remaining margarine to pan and heat until melted. Mix in coated liver and fry quickly on both sides until brown — 4 to 5 minutes.

5. Return onion and celery to pan then stir in stock, tomato purée, parsley and seasonings. Bring to the boil, cover and simmer for 15 minutes.

6. Meanwhile, blanch potato slices by simmering in boiling salted water for 6 minutes. Drain.

7. Spoon liver mixture into greased dish. Arrange potatoes in a layer over the top then sprinkle with cheese. Cook, uncovered, near top of oven for 30 minutes. Flash under a hot grill to brown and accompany with seasonal green vegetables.

Pork Chop Suey

Serves 4

Leftovers from a joint of pork take well to this treatment — livelier than sandwiches! Serve with rice or noodles.

2 tbsps salad oil
12oz (350g) cold cooked pork, cut into thin strips
4oz (125g) celery, well-scrubbed and thinly sliced
4oz (125g) onions, peeled and cut into wafer-thin slices
4oz (125g) green pepper, deseeded and cut into strips
1½oz (40g) fresh ginger, peeled and finely chopped
1 can (8oz or 228g) water chestnuts, drained and sliced
1 can (8oz or 228g) bamboo shoots, drained and sliced
1 can (10oz or 280g) bean sprouts, drained
2 level tbsps cornflour
2 tbsps light soy sauce
½ pint (275ml) chicken stock
1 tbsp Hoi Sin sauce (Chinese barbecue sauce)
1 tbsp chilli sauce

1. Heat oil in a large frying pan or wok until sizzling. Add pork, celery, onions, pepper, ginger, water chestnuts, bamboo shoots and bean sprouts. Stir-fry briskly for 5 minutes.

2. Work in cornflour then add remaining ingredients. Bring to the boil, stirring, and cook very quickly for 2 minutes. Serve straight away.

VEGETARIAN IDEAS

Tomato, Cheese and Pepper Pizza

Makes 4

Individual pizzas made with wholemeal flour and appetizingly topped with a tomato sauce, green peppers and optional olives.

Pizza Base
8oz (225g) wholemeal flour
3 level tsps baking powder
½ level tsp salt
1oz (25g) butter or margarine
1oz (25g) white vegetable cooking fat
¼ pint (150ml) cold milk

Tomato Sauce
1 can (5oz or 142g) tomato purée
2 tbsps salad oil
1 garlic clove, peeled and crushed
2 level tsps basil
¼ level tsp salt

Topping
8oz (225g) green pepper, deseeded and coarsely chopped
6oz (175g) Mozzarella cheese, grated
20 to 28 black olives (optional)

1. Lightly grease 2 large baking trays. Set oven to 200°C (400°F), gas mark 6.

2. For pizza base, tip first 3 ingredients into a bowl. Add fats and rub in finely.

3. Add milk in one go then draw mixture together with a fork. Turn out onto a lightly floured surface and knead quickly until smooth.

4. Divide dough into 4 pieces and roll each into a 6″ (15cm) round. Place on baking trays and, with finger and thumb, form a lip round edge of each to hold the filling. Leave in the cool temporarily.

5. For tomato sauce, mix all ingredients listed together well and spread over pizzas.

6. Cover peppers with boiling water and leave to stand for 3 minutes. Drain and rinse under cold water. Wipe dry in a cloth.

7. Scatter over tomato sauce then sprinkle with cheese. Stud with olives if used.

8. Bake one shelf above and one shelf below oven centre for 25 minutes, changing position of trays halfway through baking. Serve straight from the oven.

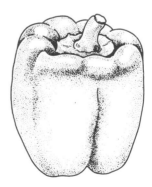

Curried Onion Patties

Makes 6

Typical packed lunch or picnic food, these tasty patties are made with a bubbly cottage cheese pastry.

4oz (125g) cottage cheese
4oz (125g) butter, taken from the refrigerator
  and coarsely grated
4oz (125g) wholemeal flour
¼ level tsp salt
½ level tsp paprika
1 tbsp salad oil
8oz (225g) onions, peeled and finely chopped
1 level tbsp curry powder
1 Grade 5 or 6 egg, beaten

1. Grease a baking tray. Preheat oven to 220°C (425°F), gas mark 7.

2. Put cottage cheese into a mixing bowl and knead until smooth with butter, flour, salt and paprika. Wrap in clingfilm or foil and refrigerate for a half hour.

3. Heat oil in a pan. Add onions and curry powder. Fry gently for 7 to 10 minutes until light golden brown. Cool.

4. Roll out pastry thinly. Cut into 12 rounds with a 3½″ (9cm) biscuit cutter.

5. Place 6 of the rounds onto prepared tray. Top with equal amounts of onion mixture. Brush edges with egg then place remaining pastry rounds on top. Pinch edges well together to seal.

6. Make a slit in the top of each pattie to allow steam to escape then brush with rest of egg.

7. Bake towards top of oven for 20 minutes or until a warm golden brown. Remove from oven and cool on a wire rack.

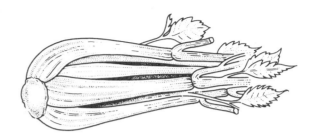

Vegetable Lattice Pie

Serves 4 to 6

A substantial pie, filled with goodness.

Pastry
8oz (225g) wholemeal flour
4oz (125g) mixture of margarine and white vegetable
  cooking fat
about 3 to 4 tbsps cold water to mix

Filling
1 14oz (400g) can tomatoes
1 garlic clove, peeled and crushed
2 level tbsps tomato purée
1 level tsp dark brown soft sugar
1 level tbsp paprika
1 level tsp oregano
6oz (175g) cauliflower florets
6oz (175g) carrots, peeled and cut into small dice
6oz (175g) onions, peeled and thinly sliced
6oz (175g) celery, well-scrubbed and thinly sliced
1 14oz (400g) can chick peas, well-drained
1 rounded tbsp chopped chives
1 rounded tbsp chopped parsley
salt and pepper to taste

Topping
1 Grade 4 egg
1 level tbsp poppy or sesame seeds

1. For pastry, tip flour into a bowl. Add fats and rub in finely. Using a fork, mix to a stiff paste with water.

2. Knead quickly until smooth on lightly floured surface. Wrap in clingfilm or foil and refrigerate temporarily.

3. For filling, drain tomatoes, place in saucepan and crush against sides. Add garlic, purée, sugar, paprika and oregano.

4. Simmer for 5 minutes over low heat. Leave aside for time being. Set oven to 200°C (400°F), Gas 6.

5. Put cauliflower, carrots, onions and celery into a separate pan. Cover with cold water. Bring to boil, leave uncovered and simmer for 7 minutes. Drain and cool.

6. Add to tomato mixture in pan then stir in chick peas, chives and parsley. Season to taste with salt and pepper then transfer to a 2 pint (1.2 litre) pie dish with rim.

7. Moisten rim with water. Roll out pastry 1″ (2½cm) larger all the way round than top of dish. Line rim with strips of pastry, cut from trimmings.

8. Moisten with water then cover with pastry lid, pressing edges of lining strips and pastry lid well together to seal.

9. Gather up rest of trimmings then re-roll and cut into narrow strips. Brush pastry lid with egg and arrange strips, in a lattice design, on top.

10. Brush with more egg, sprinkle with poppy or sesame seeds and bake just above oven centre for 35 to 40 minutes or until golden brown. Serve straight away with jacket potatoes and a green salad.

Redskin Flan

Serves 4

A mellow, curried leek filling is the surprise package in this off-beat flan with its orange-coloured pastry.

2 tbsps salad oil
8oz (225g) leeks, trimmed, well-washed, thinly sliced
6oz (175g) wholemeal flour
1 level tbsp Tandoori spice mixture
½ level tsp salt
3oz (75g) mixture of margarine and white
*   vegetable cooking fat*
6 tsps cold water
3 Grade 3 eggs
½ pint (275ml) milk
2 level tsps garam masala
¼ level tsp salt

1. Preheat oven to 200°C (400°F), gas mark 6.

2. Heat oil in pan. Add leeks and fry until golden, allowing about 10 minutes. Cool.

3. For pastry, place flour, Tandoori spice mixture and salt into a mixing bowl. Add fats and rub in until mixture resembles fine breadcrumbs. Using a fork, mix to a stiff dough with water.

4. Turn out onto a lightly floured surface and knead quickly until smooth. Roll out thinly and use to line a 8½″ (22cm) flan ring standing on a greased baking tray.

5. Cover base with fried leeks. Lightly whisk together eggs, milk, garam masala and salt. Pour over leeks.

6. Bake in oven centre for 10 minutes. Reduce heat to 160°C (325°F), gas mark 3 and cook for a further 25 to 35 minutes when filling should be set.

7. Cut into wedges and serve warm or cold.

Curried Egg and Tomato Scramble

Serves 2

A lively way with scrambled egg, perfect for lunch or supper.

4 Grade 3 eggs
1 level tbsp Madras curry powder
4 tbsps milk
¼ level tsp salt
¼ level tsp paprika
¼ level tsp turmeric
1oz (25g) butter or margarine
4oz (125g) blanched tomatoes, skinned and
coarsely chopped

1. Break eggs into a bowl. Add curry powder, milk, salt, paprika and turmeric. Beat well together.

2. Melt butter or margarine in a pan. Add egg mixture and stir over a medium heat until half set. Add tomatoes. Continue to cook until thickened, stirring. Serve on freshly made toast.

Beer Rarebits

Makes 4

An old English favourite lunch or supper dish.

1oz (25g) butter or margarine, softened
6oz (175g) Cheddar cheese, grated
1 level tsp prepared English mustard
¼ level tsp nutmeg
pinch of salt
¼ tsp Worcestershire sauce
2 tbsps beer (stout is best)
4 large slices wholemeal bread

1. Mix together butter or margarine, cheese, mustard, nutmeg, salt, Worcestershire sauce and beer.

2. Toast bread on one side only. Spread cheese mixture over untoasted sides and grill until brown, allowing about 2 minutes. Serve straight away.

Spiced Cheese on Crumpets

Makes 6

Very much a weekend special and best washed down with cool beer or vintage cider.

1oz (25g) butter or margarine, softened
6oz (175g) red Leicester cheese, grated
2 level tsps finely chopped chives
1 level tsp garam masala
1 level tsp prepared English mustard
¼ tsp Worcestershire sauce
pinch of salt
2 tbsps milk
6 crumpets

1. Mix together butter or margarine, cheese, chives, garam masala, mustard, Worcestershire sauce, salt and milk.

2. Toast crumpets lightly on both sides. Spread cheese mixture over the holey surfaces.

3. Place under grill and heat until cheese mixture is bubbly and beginning to turn golden brown; about 1½ minutes.

Opposite: Sweet and Sour Noodles (page 61).

Opposite: Exotic Fruit Kebabs (page 70).

Deep Dish Pizzas

Makes 3

Typically North American, these are generously proportioned pizzas with a thin, crusty dough.

Dough
1 level tsp castor sugar
½ pint (275ml) warm water
1½ level tsp dried yeast
1lb (450g) strong plain white flour
1 level tsp salt
½oz (15g) butter or margarine
1½ tsp salad oil

Filling
1 can (1lb 12oz or 795g) tomatoes, well-drained
1 level tsp oregano
1 level tsp basil
3 level tbsps tomato purée
½ level tbsp dark brown soft sugar
½ level tsp salt
1lb (450g) Mozzarella cheese, grated
8oz (225g) mushrooms, sliced and lightly fried in
*   ½oz (15g) butter or margarine*
6oz (175g) grated Parmesan cheese
6 tsps salad oil

1. For dough, dissolve sugar in warm water. Sprinkle yeast on top and leave to stand for 15 to 20 minutes or until mixture froths up and looks like a glass of beer with a head.

2. Sift flour and salt into a mixing bowl. Add butter or margarine and rub in finely. Pour in yeast liquid and work to a firm dough with fingers. Turn out onto a lightly floured surface and knead for 10 minutes until dough is smooth, elastic and no longer sticky.

3. Transfer dough to a lightly oiled bowl. Cover loosely with a piece of oiled clingfilm and stand in a warm place until double in size.

4. Preheat oven to 240°C (475°F), gas mark 9. Lightly grease 3 × 8″ (20cm) sandwich tins.

5. Remove dough from bowl. Knead for 2 minutes then divide equally into 3 pieces. Place in tins and leave to rest for 4 minutes as this enables dough to be handled more easily.

6. Using knuckles, spread dough over base and up sides of each tin to form a very thin shell. Prick bases all over with a fork. Bake for exactly 4 minutes. Remove from oven and brush surfaces lightly with oil to give a crisper crust.

7. Place tomatoes, herbs, purée, sugar and salt in a bowl. Mash well to combine ingredients and break down tomatoes.

8. Sprinkle grated Mozzarella cheese liberally over pizza crusts. Coat with tomato topping then scatter mushrooms on top. Sprinkle the grated Parmesan cheese over surfaces.

9. Trickle 2 teaspoons of oil over each then bake towards top of oven for 20 minutes. Carefully ease out of tins and serve straight away.

Pastry Pizza with Onions

Serves 4

A robust, hearty pizza, made unusually with brown pastry and packed with onions.

8oz (225g) wholemeal flour
1 level tsp baking powder
½ level tsp salt
4oz (125g) mixture of margarine and white
*   vegetable cooking fat*
10 to 12 tsps cold water
1 5oz (142ml) can tomato purée
4 tbsps salad oil
1 garlic clove, peeled and crushed
2 level tsps basil
½ level tsp sage
¼ level tsp salt
1lb (450g) onions, peeled and thinly sliced
4oz (125g) Mozzarella cheese, grated
4oz (125g) Cheddar cheese, grated

1. Lightly grease a 12½″ × 9″ (32 × 23cm) Swiss roll tin. Preheat oven to 200°C (400°F), gas mark 6.

2. Place flour in a bowl. Sift in baking powder and salt. Add fats and rub in finely. Using a fork, mix to a stiff dough with water.

3. Turn out onto a lightly floured surface and knead quickly until smooth. Roll out and use to line base and sides of prepared tin. Cover and refrigerate temporarily.

4. Place tomato purée, 2 tablespoons oil, garlic, basil, sage and salt in a pan. Stir over medium heat for 3 to 4 minutes until oil is absorbed. Cool slightly.

5. Heat remaining oil in separate pan. Add onions and fry for 10 to 15 minutes, or until a warm golden brown.

6. Spread pastry base with tomato sauce. Scatter onions on top then sprinkle with cheeses. Bake towards top of oven for 25 minutes.

7. Cut into 4 portions and serve straight away.

Double Cheese Pizza

Serves 4

Simply assembled, this pizza is baked in 1 tin and cut into portions for serving.

Pizza Dough Base and Tomato Sauce as given in recipe for Tomato, Cheese and Pepper Pizza (page 45).

8oz (225g) cottage cheese
2 level tbsps finely chopped parsley
1 level tsp oregano
1 can (7½oz or 213g) sliced mushrooms, drained
3 fresh chillies (½oz or 15g), slit, deseeded, chopped
6oz (175g) Mozzarella cheese

1. Lightly grease a 12½″ × 8″ (32 × 23cm) Swiss roll tin. Preheat oven to 200°C (400°F), gas mark 6.

2. Roll out dough fairly thinly and use to line base and sides of tin. Spread with tomato sauce then top with cottage cheese.

3. Sprinkle with parsley, oregano and mushrooms. Cover chillies with boiling water and stand for 3 minutes. Drain thoroughly and scatter over mushrooms with the Mozzarella cheese.

4. Bake towards top of oven for 25 minutes. Cut into 4 portions and serve straight away.

Vegetable Curry

Serves 6

A warm-hearted curry meal for winter and spring.

2 tbsps salad oil
8oz (225g) onions, peeled and finely chopped
1 level tbsp Madras curry powder
2 chillies, deseeded and finely chopped
1 garlic clove, crushed
10oz (275g) unpeeled courgettes, washed and sliced
 into ¼" (5mm) slices
8oz (225g) Brussels sprouts, peeled and quartered
8oz (225g) well-scrubbed celery, thinly sliced
 into diagonal strips
4oz (125g) trimmed and well-washed leeks, sliced
 thinly into diagonal strips
1 14oz (400g) can tomatoes
¾ pint (450ml) vegetable stock
1 level tsp salt
1 level tsp sugar
¼ level tsp ground coriander
1 level tsp fennel seeds
seeds from 2 opened-out cardamom pods

1. Heat oil in a heavy-based and large pan. Add onions and curry powder and fry over medium heat until light brown, allowing about 10 minutes.

2. Add chillies and garlic. Cook for a further 1 minute.

3. Stir in courgettes, sprouts, celery and leeks. Fry for 2 minutes, stirring all the time.

4. Add canned tomatoes, stock, salt, sugar, coriander, and fennel and cardamom seeds. Bring to the boil, cover then simmer for 45 minutes.

5. Serve with freshly cooked white or brown rice forked with 2 level teaspoons of paprika and 1 heaped teaspoon of butter or margarine.

6. Accompany with side dishes (sambals) of plain yoghurt sprinkled with caraway seeds, cut-up tomatoes sprinkled with freshly chopped mint or chives and a dish of chutney.

Pub Stuff Pizzas

Serves 4 generously

Double crust pizzas which go down extremely well with a glass of chilled beer or some cooled rosé wine.

Pizza Dough Base (double quantity) and Tomato Sauce as given in recipe for Tomato, Cheese and Pepper Pizza.

1 11oz (300g) can sliced mushrooms, drained
6oz (175g) Cheddar cheese, grated
1 Grade 4 egg, beaten

1. Grease 2 baking trays. Preheat oven to 220°C (425°F), gas mark 7.

2. Divide dough into 8 pieces and roll each into a 6" (15cm) round. Place 2 rounds on each baking tray.

3. Spread with tomato sauce to within ½" (1.25cm) of edges. Pile with mushrooms and cheese.

4. Brush edges with egg, cover with remaining rounds and seal tops and bottoms well together.

5. Brush tops with more egg then bake one shelf above and one shelf below oven centre for 25 minutes, reversing position of trays halfway through baking. Eat straight away.

VEGETABLE DISHES AND SALADS

Red Cabbage and Apples

Serves 8 to 10

A classic Central and North European sweet-sour cabbage dish, a wonderful partner for sausages, bacon, pork, duck, game and all manner of nut roasts and cutlets.

2lb (900g) red cabbage, finely shredded
8 juniper berries, crushed
¾ pint (450ml) boiling water
1 level tsp salt
8oz (225g) onions, peeled and finely chopped
8oz (225g) cooking apples, peeled, cored,
*   coarsely chopped*
2oz (50g) dark brown soft sugar
1 level tsp caraway seeds
1 bouquet garni bag
1 level tbsp cornflour
3 tbsps malt vinegar
1 tbsp cold water

1. Place red cabbage, crushed junipers, ¼ pint (150ml) boiling water and salt into a large saucepan. Bring to the boil, cover and simmer for 30 minutes.

2. Stir in remaining water with onions, apples, sugar, caraway seeds and bouquet garni bag. Cover and cook very gently for 1½ hours, stirring frequently.

3. Remove bouquet garni bag. Blend cornflour smoothly with vinegar and cold water. Stir into cabbage and cook, uncovered, for 10 minutes. Stir often to prevent sticking.

Tip
Refrigerate leftovers, well covered, and re-heat gently before serving. For a more mature flavour, make one day for the next.

Sweet and Sour Celery and Potato

Serves 4

Designed for omelettes and fried eggs, this vegetable dish is a happy combination and unusually uses sweet potatoes.

1 tsp salad oil
12oz (350g) sweet potatoes or yams, grated
6oz (175g) celery, well-scrubbed and cut into
*   matchstick-sized pieces*
2 level tsps cornflour
¼ pint (150ml) chicken or vegetable stock
1 tbsp malt vinegar
2 tsps soy sauce
¼ level tsp nutmeg

1. Heat oil in pan. Add potatoes and celery then stir-fry over a high heat for 3 minutes.

2. Blend cornflour with 2 tablespoons of stock. Pour into vegetables. Blend in remaining stock, vinegar, soy sauce and nutmeg.

3. Bring to the boil, cover and simmer for 5 minutes, stirring frequently.

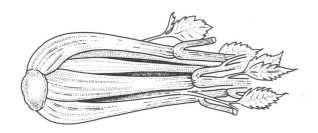

Potato and Cheese Soufflé

Serves 4

With a green salad tossed in a well-flavoured French dressing, this is haute cuisine at its best.

1lb (450g) potatoes, peeled and quartered
boiling salted water
4oz (125g) Cheddar cheese, grated
4 Grade 3 eggs, separated
1 level tsp powder mustard
½ level tsp salt

1. Well grease a 2½ pint (1.5 litre) soufflé dish. Preheat oven to 190°C (375°F), gas mark 5.

2. Cook potatoes in boiling salted water for 15 to 20 minutes or until tender. Drain well.

3. Place in food processor and blend until smooth.

4. Add cheese, egg yolks, mustard and salt. Blend again. Spoon into bowl.

5. Separately, beat egg whites to a stiff snow. Using a large metal spoon, swiftly fold into potato mixture.

6. Pour into prepared dish. Bake for 45 minutes until soufflé is risen and golden. Do *not* open the oven door and serve straight away as a soufflé falls very quickly.

Blue Cheese Soufflé

Serves 4

Use Lymeswold blue cheese instead of Cheddar.

Curried Potato and Carrots

Serves 4 to 6

Eat with hot baby pancakes or dropped scones for a main meal. Alternatively, serve with chicken dishes.

1oz (25g) butter or margarine
1 tsp salad oil
4oz (125g) onions, peeled and finely chopped
1 garlic clove, peeled and crushed
1 level tbsp mild curry powder
2 level tbsps flour
1 rounded tbsp tomato purée
1 level tbsp finely chopped fresh coriander
1 level tbsp mango and ginger chutney
1 level tsp granulated sugar
1 tsp lemon juice
½ level tsp salt
½ pint (275ml) vegetable stock or water
1lb (450g) carrots, peeled and cut into
*   ¼" (6mm) slices*
1lb (450g) potatoes, peeled and cut into
*   ½" (1.25cm) cubes*

1. Heat butter or margarine in a pan with oil. Add onions, garlic and curry powder. Fry until golden brown, allowing about 10 minutes.

2. Stir in flour and cook for 2 minutes. Add tomato purée, coriander, chutney, sugar, lemon juice, salt, stock or water and carrots. Bring to the boil, stirring.

3. Cover and simmer for 30 minutes. Add potatoes and continue cooking, covered, for a further 15 minutes.

Leeks Braised in Cinzano

Serves 4

Easy and good, this is just the thing to serve with meat and poultry.

10 small leeks, trimmed with 1" (2.5cm)
  green remaining
¼ pint (150ml) Cinzano
1 small garlic clove, peeled and crushed
¼ level tsp salt

1. Leave leeks whole and wash throughly. Place in a shallow pan with Cinzano, crushed garlic and salt.
2. Bring to the boil, cover and simmer for 45 minutes. Turn occasionally.

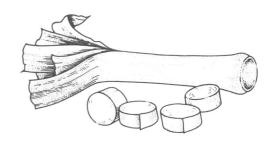

Mushroom Starter Salads

Serves 4

An amiable beginning to any kind of meal.

1 level tbsp mild mustard powder
3 tbsps salad oil
1½ tbsp wine vinegar
1½ level tbsp finely chopped parsley
1½ level tbsps finely chopped chives
1 level tsp castor sugar
12oz (350g) mushrooms, washed, dried, thinly sliced

1. In medium bowl, whisk together mustard, oil, vinegar, parsley, chives and sugar.
2. Add mushrooms and toss. Cover and refrigerate for 2 to 3 hours. Spoon into dishes and serve.

Celeriac in Cheese Sauce

Serves 4

A warming lunch or supper dish made with a subtle-tasting winter vegetable.

1¼lb (575g) celeriac, thickly peeled and cut into
  ½" (1.25cm) cubes
boiling salted water
2 tsps lemon juice
1oz (25g) butter or margarine
1oz (25g) plain flour
½ pint (275ml) milk
1 tsp Worcestershire sauce
2 level tsps finely chopped chives
1 level tsp mustard powder
½ level tsp paprika
¼ level tsp salt
4oz (125g) Cheddar cheese, grated

1. Cook celeriac, covered, in boiling salted water with lemon juice for 10 minutes. Drain.
2. Melt butter or margarine in a saucepan. Add flour and cook for 2 minutes, stirring. Blend in milk. Bring to the boil, stirring, then mix in Worcestershire sauce, chives, mustard, paprika and salt. Simmer for 1 minute.

3. Remove pan from heat and stir in half the cheese until melted. Add celeriac and heat through. Turn into a greased heatproof dish, sprinkle rest of cheese on top and brown under a hot grill.

Mooli in Caper and Parsley Vinaigrette

Serves 2

A sound salad which goes happily with meat, poultry and vegetarian dishes.

10oz (275g) mooli (white radish or rettich), peeled and cut
into ¼" (6mm) slices
boiling salted water
2 tbsps salad oil
1 tbsp tarragon vinegar
2 level tbsps finely chopped parsley
1 level tsp finely chopped capers
¼ level tsp salt
pepper to taste
2 level tbsps chopped parsley for sprinkling
over the top

1. Simmer mooli, covered, for 10 minutes in boiling salted water. Drain.

2. Whisk together remaining ingredients except parsley. Add hot mooli and toss over and over in the dressing.

3. Leave until cool then cover and refrigerate. Chill for about 2 to 3 hours. Sprinkle with parsley before serving.

Saffron Carrots with Lemon

Serves 4

Beautifully aromatic and warmly-coloured, this makes an excellent accompaniment for roast veal and chicken.

1lb (450g) carrots
1oz (25g) butter or margarine
6 saffron strands
¼ level tsp salt
2 level tsps finely grated orange or lemon peel

1. Peel and wash carrots then cut into wafer-thin slices.

2. Melt butter or margarine in a pan. Add all remaining ingredients. Cover. Simmer over a low heat for 15 minutes.

3. Stir once or twice to prevent sticking.

Creamed Kolocassi

Serves 4

A root vegetable similar to potatoes, kolocassi has a unique flavour and warming texture, superb with any kind of beef stew. Note that it is very starchy.

1lb (450g) kolocassi, peeled, washed, stump removed, diced
cold water to cover
½ level tsp salt
½ tsp lemon juice
½oz (15g) butter or margarine
2 tbsps milk or cream
⅛ tsp grated nutmeg
salt and pepper to taste

1. Put kolocassi into a saucepan. Add cold water to cover then mix in salt and lemon juice.

2. Bring to the boil, lower heat and cover. Simmer for 25 to 30 minutes or until tender.

3. Drain and mash. Add all remaining ingredients and beat over a low heat until well-creamed. Serve straight away.

Celeriac Salad

Serves 4

Tried first in North Germany, I am now a devotee of this handsome salad which is so appetizing with eggs, poultry and fish.

1¼lb (575g) celeriac, thickly peeled and cut into
½" (1.25cm) cubes
boiling salted water
2 tsps lemon juice
2 tbsps salad oil
1 tbsp malt vinegar
2 level tsps Continental mustard
1 level tsp caraway seeds
¼ level tsp salt
pepper to taste

1. Cook celeriac, covered, in boiling salted water with lemon juice for 15 to 20 minutes or until tender. Drain.
2. Whisk together all remaining ingredients. Add hot celeriac and toss over and over in the dressing.
3. Cover and cool. Serve at room temperature.

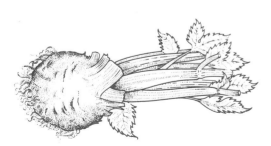

Celeriac and Cucumber Salad

Serves 4

A crunchy salad with a refreshing tang.

Peel 4oz (125g) cucumber and cut into ¼" (6mm) cubes. Stir into cooled celeriac salad (above). For a decorative touch, sprinkle with mustard and cress.

Heavenly Moon Vegetables

Serves 6

Fashionably oriental, this is a mix of unusual vegetables and perfect as part of a Chinese meal ensemble.

2 tsps salad oil
4oz (125g) onions, peeled and finely chopped
2 level tsps plain flour
10oz (275g) mooli (white radish or rettich),
peeled and grated
1 8oz (228g) can water chestnuts, drained and thinly
sliced
½ pint (275ml) water
1 tbsp light soy sauce
1 tsp dark soy sauce
½ level tsp 5-star spice
1 vegetable stock cube

1. Heat oil in pan. Add onions and fry for 10 minutes until golden.
2. Stir in flour and cook for 1 minute.
3. Mix in mooli, water chestnuts, water, both soy sauces and spice. Crumble in stock cube then bring to the boil. Cover. Simmer for 30 minutes.

GRAINS AND PASTA

Trattoria Noodles

Serves 4

Make this and imagine you're on holiday, eating out in a small, candlelit restaurant!

1oz (25g) butter or margarine
2 garlic cloves, peeled and crushed
12oz (350g) mushrooms, trimmed and thinly sliced
1 level tbsp flour
½ pint (275ml) chicken stock
3 tbsps dry white wine
2 level tbsps tomato purée
1 level tsp basil
8oz (225g) cold, cooked chicken, cut into narrow strips
seasoning to taste
12oz (350g) wholewheat or plain noodles
4 pints (2.5 litres) boiling water
1½ level tsp salt
grated Parmesan cheese

1. Heat butter or margarine in a pan. Add garlic and mushrooms and fry fairly briskly for 5 minutes, turning frequently.

2. Stir in flour. Cook for 1 minute then add stock, wine, purée, basil, chicken and seasoning to taste. Cover pan and simmer for 15 minutes over medium heat, stirring from time to time.

3. Meanwhile, cook noodles in boiling water and salt for about 10 minutes, keeping pan two-thirds covered with lid. Drain and toss with the chicken mixture.

4. Spoon out onto warm plates and sprinkle each with Parmesan cheese.

Spaghetti 'Kedgeree'

Serves 4

So often the simplest dishes are often the best and this is an added bonus on any buffet table, be it for breakfast, brunch or supper.

12oz (350g) smoked haddock or cod fillet
cold water
4 pints (2.5 litres) boiling water
8oz (225g) pasta shells
1 level tsp salt
2oz (50g) butter or margarine
2 level tbsps chopped parsley
1 level tsp tarragon
3 Grade 3 eggs, beaten
freshly milled black pepper to taste

1. Put haddock or cod into a pan and cover with cold water. Bring to the boil and drain. Repeat once more to reduce saltiness. Cover fish with more cold water and cook for 10 minutes. Drain and flake, taking care to remove any bones.

2. Pour boiling water into a pan. Add pasta shells and salt. Two-thirds cover and boil for 10 minutes. Drain and return to pan.

3. Add butter or margarine, half the parsley, tarragon, fish, beaten eggs and freshly milled pepper to taste. Toss with 2 spoons until the heat of the pasta scrambles the eggs.

4. Transfer to 4 warm plates and sprinkle with remaining parsley. Eat with brown bread or rolls.

Far Away Spaghetti with Meatball Sauce

Serves 4

Imitation Chinese for amateurs! Serve with oriental noodles or rice.

Meatballs
1lb (450g) lean minced beef
2oz (50g) soft brown breadcrumbs
1 garlic clove, peeled and crushed
1½ level tbsp Hoi Sin sauce
  (Chinese barbecue sauce)
½ level tsp salt
⅛ level tsp chilli powder
pepper to taste

Sauce
3 tbsps salad oil
8oz (225g) onions, peeled and finely chopped
8oz (225g) Chinese leaves, washed, halved lengthwise,
  finely shredded
1 level tbsp cornflour
¼ pint (150ml) cold water } *blended*
¼ pint (150ml) boiling water
1 beef or chicken stock cube, crumbled
½ level tsp salt
¼ level tsp caraway seeds
pepper to taste

Spaghetti
2 pints (1.2 litres) water
1 level tsp salt
6oz (175g) wholewheat spaghetti

1. Place all meatball ingredients into a bowl and mix thoroughly. Roll into 16 even-sized balls.

2. For sauce, heat oil in pan. Add onions and fry for about 10 minutes until golden brown.

3. Stir in remaining sauce ingredients and bring to the boil. Add meatballs and cover. Simmer gently for 30 minutes, carefully stirring twice or three times to prevent sticking.

4. After meatballs have been cooking for a quarter hour, prepare spaghetti. Bring water and salt to the boil. Add spaghetti, two-thirds cover pan and boil for 12 to 15 minutes. Drain.

5. Place spaghetti into a warm serving dish. Spoon meatballs and sauce on top. Serve straight away.

Chilli Rice

Serves 4

An easy-to-make rice dish with a bit of fire in it. Serve hot with roast lamb or poultry, cold with salads containing eggs and cheese.

1 tbsp salad oil
8oz (225g) onions, peeled and finely chopped
2oz (50g) chillies, deseeded and cut into narrow strips
6oz (175g) Italian style risotto rice
12fl oz (350ml) vegetable stock
½ level tsp salt
4oz (125g) cottage cheese

1. Heat oil in a pan. Add onions and chillies. Fry gently until golden, allowing about 10 to 15 minutes.

2. Stir in rice, stock and salt. Bring to the boil, lower heat and cover. Cook for 20 to 25 minutes or until all the liquid has evaporated and rice grains are tender.

3. Remove from heat and fork in cottage cheese. Use as desired.

Christmas Pasta

Serves 6

A pretty accompaniment to roast turkey or gammon.

1oz (25g) butter or margarine
4oz (125g) onions, peeled and chopped
2oz (50g) carrots, peeled and grated
1oz (25g) green pepper, deseeded and chopped
8oz (225g) pasta bows or shells
½ pint (275ml) boiling apple juice
½ pint (275ml) boiling water
1 level tsp salt

1. Heat butter or margarine until foaming. Add prepared vegetables and fry over medium heat until pale gold. Keep pan covered throughout.

2. Stir in pasta, apple juice, water and salt. Bring to the boil and lower heat.

3. Cover and simmer for about 12 to 15 minutes, stirring once with a spoon.

Christmas Bacon Salad

Serves 6

For a more substantial dish which can be served as a main course, add 12oz (350g) cooked, diced gammon at the same time as the apple juice, water and salt. Accompany with a crisp salad.

Spaghetti with Spring Onion Cream Sauce

Serves 4

A fine starter in true Italian fashion.

12oz (350g) wholewheat spaghetti
3 pints (1.75 litres) boiling water
1½ level tsps salt
2oz (50g) butter or margarine
3oz (75g) spring onions, trimmed and chopped
1 level tbsp flour
¼ pint (150ml) single cream
2 level tsp dried dill weed
⅛ level tsp nutmeg
salt and pepper to taste
4 rounded tbsps grated Swiss cheese for sprinkling
over the top

1. Cook spaghetti in boiling salted water for 12 to 15 minutes, keeping pan two-thirds covered throughout.

2. Meanwhile, melt half the butter or margarine in a saucepan, add spring onions and fry for 5 minutes or until soft. Work in flour and cook for a further minute.

3. Gradually blend in cream, followed by dill weed, nutmeg and salt and pepper to taste. Cook, stirring all the time, until sauce comes to the boil and thickens. Simmer for 1 minute. Remove from heat.

4. Drain spaghetti, return to pan and toss with remaining butter or margarine. Add onion sauce and toss again.

5. Transfer to 4 warm plates and serve each portion sprinkled with cheese.

Bacon Spaghetti with Spring Onion Cream Sauce

Serves 4

Make as previous recipe but instead of cheese, sprinkle each portion with 2 heaped tablespoons crisply fried and well-drained chopped streaky bacon.

Brown Rice and Vegetable Pot Pourri

Serves 8

A complete meal in itself, appetizing with sauce made from a can of condensed asparagus soup, heated with 4 tablespoons of milk and the same amount of white wine.

8oz (225g) brown rice, washed
4 pints (2.25 litres) boiling water
1 level tsp salt
2 tbsps salad oil
8oz (225g) potatoes, peeled and grated
6oz (175g) parsnips, peeled and grated
6oz (175g) swede, peeled and grated
6oz (175g) carrots, peeled and grated
4oz (125g) onions, peeled and grated
6oz (175g) Chinese leaves, finely shredded
4oz (125g) well-scrubbed celery, dried and grated
½ level tsp thyme
½ level tsp basil
½ level tsp garlic salt
½ level tsp salt
pepper
1 15½oz (439g) can red kidney beans, drained
1 11½oz (326g) can sweetcorn, drained
8oz (225g) Cheddar cheese, grated

1. Put rice into a pan with boiling water and salt. Stir round and boil, covered, for 45 minutes. Drain.

2. Heat oil in separate pan until sizzling. Add vegetables, herbs and seasonings. Fry for 10 minutes, stirring frequently, until just cooked.

3. Stir cooked rice, red kidney beans, sweetcorn and half the cheese into vegetables.

4. Spread evenly into a 10" (25cm) square, shallow, well greased dish. Sprinkle with remaining cheese and brown under grill for 2 to 3 minutes.

5. Serve by spooning onto warm plates and accompany with 1 pint (575ml) white sauce, flavoured with 1 level tablespoon of each of chopped parsley, chopped fresh coriander and chopped chives. Season to taste with salt and pepper.

Sweet and Sour Noodles

Serves 4

A Chinese approach to pasta and sausagemeat — two basic ingredients which take well to dressing up.

1lb (450g) sausagemeat
1 level tsp dried herbs
1 Grade 3 egg, beaten
1 level tbsp flour
oil for frying
10oz (275g) noodles
boiling salted water
2 level tbsps cornflour
1 tbsp soy sauce
8 tbsps wine vinegar
1 tbsp molasses sugar
8oz (225g) can pineapple pieces (reserve juice)
seasoning to taste
1 large carrot, cut into thin strips
1 canned pimiento, cut into thin strips
spring onions for garnish

1. Mix the sausagemeat with herbs and shape into round meatballs. Coat with beaten egg, dust with the flour and fry in the oil until the sausagemeat is cooked through. Drain on kitchen paper.

2. Cook the noodles in plenty of boiling salted water, with a little oil added, until just tender or 'al dente'.

3. Meanwhile, make the sweet and sour sauce by blending the cornflour smoothly with the soy sauce, vinegar, molasses, sugar and pineapple juice in a saucepan and stirring until thickened and transparent.

4. Season to taste. Add the strips of carrot, pimiento and pineapple pieces. Mix well.

5. Drain the noodles and arrange around the outside of a serving dish. Place the cooked sausagemeat balls on top and coat with the sweet and sour sauce. Serve straight away. Garnish with spring onions, made into 'lilies'.

Grecian Cocktail Parcels

Makes 24

Temptations for a drinks' party.

6oz (175g) brown rice, washed
½ pint (275ml) tomato juice, brought to the boil
½ pint (275ml) boiling water
a 3" (7.5cm) length of cinnamon stick
2 level tsps finely chopped fresh mint
24 vine leaves from an 8oz (225g) packet
extra boiling water
½ pint (275ml) stock
4oz (125g) Feta chese
24 black olives

1. In a large pan, cook rice in boiling tomato juice and water, with cinnamon stick and mint, for 45 minutes. Keep pan covered throughout. Cool slightly and remove cinnamon. Drain if necessary.

2. Cook vine leaves in boiling water to cover for 5 minutes. Drain.

3. Spread vine leaves out onto a flat surface, veined sides facing upwards. Place a spoonful of rice in the centre of each then fold up to form neat parcels, completely enclosing rice.

4. Place parcels, in a single layer, in a large frying pan. Coat with stock. Two-thirds cover. Gently simmer for 15 minutes then drain and cool.

5. Cut cheese into 24 cubes of about ½" (1.25cm). Thread onto cocktail sticks with black olives then spear into vine leaf parcels. Serve lightly chilled.

Golden Wheel Summer Pasta Salad

Serves 2

A high-fibre salad which is bright, cheerful and economical.

1¾ pint (1 litre) boiling water
½ level tsp salt
5oz (150g) pasta shells
2 heaped tbsps chopped chives or spring onions
1 7.9oz (223g) can red kidney beans, drained
4oz (125g) cooked sweetcorn, drained
1 small red pepper, deseeded and finely chopped
3oz (75g) Edam cheese, cut into small cubes
2 level tbsps mayonnaise
2 level tbsps natural yoghurt
½ level tsp ground savory
seasoning to taste
lettuce leaves for lining dish

1. Pour water into a pan. Add salt and pasta shells. Cook for 7 to 10 minutes, keeping pan two-thirds covered. Drain. Tip into a mixing bowl. Cool completely.

2. Add chives or onions, kidney beans, sweetcorn, pepper and cheese. Mix in mayonnaise, yoghurt, savory and seasoning to taste. Toss with 2 spoons to mix then arrange in a shallow dish, first lined with lettuce leaves.

Curried Nut Bulgur

Serves 4 to 6

On its own or with any cooked vegetable dish, this is a tasty mix of bulgur, spices and nuts — unusual and crunchily textured.

6oz (175g) bulgur
12fl oz (350ml) water
¼ level tsp salt
2oz (50g) brazil nuts
1 garlic clove, peeled
2 tbsps salad oil
1 level tsp Madras curry powder
¼ level tsp paprika
¼ level tsp turmeric
2oz (50g) cashew nuts
½ level tsp salt

1. Wash bulgur in a fine mesh sieve. Place in a pan with water and salt. Bring to the boil, cover and simmer for 8 minutes or until water has been absorbed and bulgur is cooked.

2. Meanwhile, thinly slice brazils. Crush garlic.

3. Heat oil in a pan. Add garlic, curry powder, paprika and turmeric. Fry for 1 to 2 minutes. Stir in brazils and cashews then fry slowly for a further 10 minutes until golden brown.

4. Stir nut mixture into bulgur with salt. Serve while still hot.

Brown Rice and Liver Risotto

Serves 4 to 6

A mellow risotto threaded with shredded lettuce.

8oz (225g) brown rice
4 pints (2.25 litres) boiling water
1 level tsp salt
1 tbsp salad oil
6oz (175g) onions, peeled and finely chopped
8oz (225g) chicken livers, washed and cut into
  fairly small pieces
2oz (50g) crisp lettuce, washed and finely shredded
4fl oz (125ml) red wine
pepper to taste
half a bay leaf

1. Wash rice. Put into pan with boiling water and ½ level teaspoon of salt. Stir round and boil, covered, for 25 minutes. Drain.

2. Heat oil in separate pan. Add onions and fry over a medium heat for 10 to 15 minutes or until golden brown.

3. Add chicken livers and fry for a further 3 minutes.

4. Add lettuce, wine, rest of salt, pepper to taste and bay leaf. Bring to the boil, cover and simmer for 10 minutes. Remove bay leaf.

5. Using a fork, stir cooked rice into chicken livers and serve straight away.

Note
The risotto may be served either as a meal starter or main course. If the latter, accompany with seasonal cooked vegetables to taste.

Vermicelli with Curry Sauce

Serves 4

An economical beef curry which makes a handsome main course with the side dishes listed below.

2 tbsps salad oil
4oz (125g) onions, peeled and chopped
1lb (450g) minced beef
¼ level tsp ground turmeric
1 level tsp chilli powder
1 level tsp ground coriander
1½ level tsps ground cumin
1 8oz (250g) can tomatoes
4oz (125g) frozen peas
seasoning to taste
12oz (350g) vermicelli
boiling salted water

1. Heat oil in a pan, add onions and fry until light brown. Add the minced beef and sprinkle with the turmeric, chilli, coriander and cumin.

2. Mix well and fry for a few minutes to brown the meat. Stir in tomatoes and cook gently for 10 minutes. Add the peas and continue cooking gently for a further 10 minutes. Season to taste.

3. Meanwhile, cook vermicelli in plenty of boiling salted water until just tender or 'al dente'.

4. Drain and arrange round edge of a warmed serving dish. Pour the curry sauce into the centre and serve straight away.

5. Accompany with a selection of small side dishes such as peanuts, sliced bananas tossed in lemon juice, desiccated coconut, sliced tomatoes with chopped spring onions, sultanas, yoghurt with diced cucumber.

Banana and Raisin Rice

Serves 4 to 6

A treat with all curried dishes, or as a cold salad on the buffet table.

12fl oz (350ml) boiling water
6oz (175g) easy-cook long grain rice
½ level tsp salt
1oz (25g) butter or margarine
1 level tsp garam masala
⅛ level tsp chilli powder
3 medium bananas, peeled and thinly sliced
4oz (125g) raisins
2 level tbsps finely chopped chives

1. Pour water into a pan then add rice and salt, stir round and cover. Simmer for 12 to 15 minutes or until rice grains are tender and have absorbed all the water.

2. In separate pan, melt butter or margarine. Add garam masala and chilli powder. Cook for 1 to 2 minutes. Stir in bananas, raisins and chives then cook for a further 3 to 4 minutes.

3. Add rice and fork stir thoroughly to mix.

Banana and Raisin Rice Pudding

Serves 4 to 6

A touch of the East in this variation which can be served as a dessert.

Make as previous recipe but omit chives. Spoon cooked rice mixture into 4 dishes and top with hot milk. For a more exotic flavour, bring milk to the boil, take off heat and add the seeds from 2 opened-out cardamom pods. Leave to stand for 10 minutes, drain and bring just up to the boil.

Arabian Nights' Salad

Serves 4 to 6

Middle Eastern in mood, this bulgur salad is especially pleasing with lamb, poultry or fish dishes such as sea bass.

6oz (175g) bulgur
12fl oz (350ml) water
½ level tsp salt
2 tbsps salad oil
1 tbsp lemon juice
3 level tbsps finely chopped parsley
1 level tsp finely chopped fresh mint
1 garlic clove, peeled and crushed
16 black olives

1. Wash bulgur in a fine mesh sieve. Place in a pan with water and salt.

2. Bring to the boil and cover. Simmer for 8 minutes until water has been absorbed and bulgur is cooked through.

3. Whisk together oil, lemon juice, parsley, mint and garlic. Mix with bulgur, cover then leave to cool.

4. Stir in olives and serve as desired.

SAUCES

Peanut Sauce

Serves 6 to 8

A typically Indonesian style sauce for the pork kebabs (Saté Babi) in the meat section.

1 tbsp salad oil
6oz (175g) onions, peeled and chopped
1 garlic clove, peeled and crushed
12oz (350g) smooth peanut butter
2 level tsps light brown soft sugar
3 tsps lemon juice
1 pint (575ml) boiling water
2 tsps brown ketchup
salt and pepper to taste

1. Heat oil in a pan until sizzling. Add onions and garlic and fry until golden. Stir in peanut butter and sugar.

2. Blend in lemon juice and half the water. Bring to the boil, stirring. Mixture will look like porridge.

3. Thin down with rest of water then stir in the brown ketchup. Season to taste with salt and pepper.

Tip
Left-over sauce should be kept, covered, in a small bowl in the refrigerator up to about one week. The sauce may also be served over mixed seasonal cooked vegetables.

Curried Apple Sauce

Makes about ¾ pint (½ litre)

Well-recommended for roast pork and bacon dishes.

1½lb (675g) cooking apples
4 tbsps water
3oz (75g) light brown soft sugar
¼ level tsp extra hot curry powder
¼ level tsp turmeric

1. Peel, core and thinly slice apples. Tip into a saucepan, then add water.

2. Cover and simmer for 15 minutes or until soft and pulpy, stirring twice or three times.

3. Place apples, sugar, curry powder and turmeric into a blender or food processor and run machine until mixture forms a smooth purée.

4. Transfer to a bowl and serve cold.

Chilli Sauce for Baked Potatoes

Serves 6

Geared for the now fashionable high fibre jacket potatoes, this is a succulent sauce laced with wine.

4 tbsps salad oil
8oz (225g) onions, peeled and finely chopped
12oz (350g) lean minced beef
4 level tbsps plain flour
4 level tsps chilli seasoning (brown to purple in colour and used for chilli con carne)
2 garlic cloves, peeled and crushed
2 level tbsps tomato purée
½ pint (275ml) water
1 level tsp salt
4 tbsps red wine

1. Heat oil until sizzling in a saucepan. Add onions and fry for 10 minutes or until golden. Stir in meat and brown for 2 to 3 minutes over a fairly high heat.

2. Mix in flour and cook for a further 1 to 2 minutes.

3. Add chilli seasoning, garlic, tomato purée, water and salt.

4. Bring to the boil, cover and simmer for 40 to 45 minutes. Stir occasionally. Blend in wine.

5. To serve, cut a cross on top of 6 freshly-baked jacket potatoes. Open out by squeezing base of each with hand protected by oven glove.

6. Put onto warm plates and coat thickly with sauce.

Mushroom Sauce

Makes about ¾ pint (450ml)

Fast to make with store cupboard ingredients, and good to eat with roast poultry and grilled or fried fish.

1 10.4oz (295g) can condensed cream of mushroom soup
1 7½oz (213g) can sliced mushrooms, drained
4 tbsps milk
6 tbsps water
⅛ level tsp salt
⅛ level tsp marjoram
pepper to taste
1 tbsp medium sherry

1. Place all ingredients into a small pan. Bring to the boil, stirring continuously and simmer for 2 to 3 minutes. Use as required.

Barbecue Sauce

Makes just over ¼ pint (150ml)

A lively sauce for brushing over chops, steaks, chicken, burgers and sausages before barbecuing or grilling.

¼ pint (150ml) French dressing
3 level tbsps tomato ketchup
1 tbsp soy sauce
1 tbsp Worcestershire sauce
1 tbsp lemon juice
½ level tsp mixed herbs

1. Place all ingredients into a saucepan, bring to the boil and simmer until bubbly.

2. Remove from heat and use as required.

Hot Cheese Sauce for Baked Potatoes

Serves 6

A vegetarian's delight!

1oz (25g) butter or margarine
4oz (125g) carrots, peeled and grated
1 oz (25g) flour
½ pint (275ml) milk
1 level tsp dry mustard
2 tsps lemon juice
1 tsp Worcestershire sauce
large pinch of nutmeg
large pinch of cayenne pepper
½ level tsp marjoram
½ level tsp salt
2oz (50g) Cheddar cheese, grated
2 tbsps hot water

1. Melt butter or margarine in a saucepan. Add carrots and fry gently for 5 minutes. Stir in flour and cook for 1 to 2 minutes.

2. Blend in milk. Bring to the boil, stirring. Add mustard, lemon juice, Worcestershire sauce, nutmeg, cayenne pepper, marjoram and salt. Simmer for 2 to 3 minutes then remove from heat.

3. Add cheese and stir over minimal heat until melted. Blend in water.

4. Serve over potatoes as directed in recipe for Chilli Sauce.

Curry Sauce for Baked Potatoes

Serves 6

Another version of meat sauce, tastefully splashed with dry cider.

4 tsps salad oil
8oz (225g) onions, peeled and finely chopped
4 level tsps Madras curry powder
12oz (350g) minced beef, as lean as possible
4 level tsps plain flour
milk of 2 small coconuts made up to ½ pint (275ml)
*   with water*
2 level tbsps tomato purée
4 level tsps mango and ginger chutney
1 level tsp salt
4 tbsps dry cider

1. Heat oil in saucepan. Add onions and curry powder. Fry slowly until golden, allowing about 10 minutes. Add meat. Brown for a further 2 to 3 minutes, stirring.

2. Mix in flour and cook for 2 minutes.

3. Add coconut liquid, tomato purée, chutney and salt.

4. Bring gently to the boil and cover. Simmer for 40 to 45 minutes, stirring occasionally. Blend in cider.

5. Serve over potatoes as directed in recipe for Chilli Sauce.

Tip
When coconuts are out of season, make the milk by soaking 1oz (25g) desiccated coconut in ½ pint (275ml) plus 3 tablespoons water for half an hour. Strain and use.

Blackberry Sauce

Makes ½ pint (275ml)

Sophisticated as an accompaniment for roast duck and lightly fried or grilled chicken livers. It may also be served, while still hot, over ice cream or with steamed puddings. When cold, it can be stirred into plain yoghurt or used as an unusual sauce for fruit salad.

1lb (450g) blackberries
3oz (75g) castor sugar
1 cinnamon stick, 3" (7.5cm) in length
1 level tsp cornflour

1. Wash and drain blackberries. Put into a saucepan with sugar and cinnamon. Cover and simmer for 10 minutes. Remove cinnamon stick.

2. Rub blackberries and liquid through a sieve then make up purée to ½ pint (275ml) with extra cold water.

3. Blend 1 tablespoon purée with cornflour then mix with rest of purée.

4. Spoon into a saucepan and simmer for 2 to 3 minutes until thickened, stirring continuously.

Raspberry Sauce

Makes ½ pint (275ml)

A pleasing sauce, recommended for the same dishes as the Blackberry Sauce. It also goes well with lightly roast lamb and grilled kidneys.

Mix as Blackberry Sauce substituting raspberries for blackberries.

Brown Bread Sauce

Makes ½ pint (275ml)

A more healthy version of traditional bread sauce made with brown crumbs.

½ pints (275ml) milk (skimmed if preferred)
1 level tsp dried onion flakes
2oz (50g) brown breadcrumbs
½oz (15g) butter or margarine
⅛ level tsp salt
⅛ level tsp ground cloves
pinch cayenne pepper

1. Slowly bring milk and onion flakes to the boil. Leave to stand for 5 minutes then strain.

2. Rinse out pan. Return onion-flavoured milk with breadcrumbs, butter or margarine, salt, cloves and cayenne pepper.

3. Bring to the boil, stirring continuously, and simmer gently for 3 minutes until thickened. Keep pan half covered to prevent spluttering.

Almond Bread Sauce

Makes ½ pint (275ml)

Follow recipe for Brown Bread Sauce. Toast and crumble 1oz (25g) flaked almonds and add to sauce after it has thickened.

DESSERTS

Carambola (Star Fruit) and Pineappe Compôte

Serves 6

A new combination of ingredients makes for an outstanding but simply prepared fruit dish.

12oz (350g) pineapple, cut into small cubes
12oz (350g) carambola (approximately 2 pieces of fruit)
3oz (75g) sultanas
½ pint (275ml) white grape juice
3oz (75g) castor sugar
leaves of tansy or mint to decorate

1. Place pineapple in a pan.
2. Pare a thin strip from the edge of each point of the carambola. Remove top and bottom. Slice fruit into thin slices. Remove seeds.
3. Add carambola, sultanas and grape juice to pineapple in saucepan. Bring to the boil, cover and simmer gently for 20 minutes.
4. Remove from heat, add sugar and stir until dissolved.
5. Transfer to a serving bowl. Decorate with tansy or mint leaves.

Knights in Armour

Serves 8

Family food at its best.

8 medium thick slices of white bread
4 level tbsps lemon curd
2 Grade 3 eggs
¼ pint (150ml) milk
2oz (50g) butter or margarine
1 tbsp salad oil
1oz (25g) castor sugar
½ level tsp cinnamon } *tossed together*

1. Remove crusts from bread. Spread slices with lemon curd and sandwich together in pairs. Halve diagonally.
2. Lightly whisk together eggs and milk. Dip half the sandwiches into the egg mixture.
3. Heat butter and oil in a large frying pan until hot. Add dipped sandwiches and fry until crisp and brown on both sides, turning twice.
4. Drain on crumpled kitchen paper and sprinkle with cinnamon sugar. Repeat with remaining sandwiches. Serve hot.

Louisiana Sweet Potato Pie

Serves 6

A warmly fragrant pie from North America's deep south.

2lb (900g) sweet potatoes
4oz (125g) castor sugar
3oz (75g) butter or margarine
2 Grade 3 eggs
1 tsp vanilla essence
¼ level tsp mace
3fl oz (75ml) milk

Topping
2oz (50g) butter or margarine, melted
6oz (175g) demerara sugar
3oz (75g) plain flour
4oz (125g) brazil nuts, chopped

1. Preheat oven to 180°C (350°F), gas mark 4.

2. Peel potatoes and cut into large pieces. Put into a pan, add cold water to cover and bring to the boil. Cover pan with lid then boil steadily for 15 to 20 minutes or until potatoes are soft. Drain and finely mash.

3. Beat in sugar, butter or margarine, eggs, vanilla essence, mace and milk.

4. Spread evenly into baking dish measuring 11" × 9" (28 × 23cm).

5. Mix together topping ingredients and sprinkle over pie.

6. Bake for 25 minutes until the crumbs are just beginning to brown.

7. Spoon out of the dish and serve with thick cream.

Exotic Fruit Kebabs

Makes 4

approximately 3 each peaches, green apples, bananas and oranges (use fruit that is slightly under-ripe)
a few tbsps lemon juice
3oz (75g) glacé cherries
a little jellied cranberry sauce
mixed spice for sprinkling

1. Remove the stones from the peaches and core the apples. Cut each fruit into eight pieces.

2. Place in bowl with a little lemon juice and stir so that each piece of fruit is covered to prevent browning. Peel the bananas and cut into 1" (2.5cm). Repeat with oranges.

3. Thread the fruits alternately on to four kebab skewers, placing a glacé cherry at intervals as desired.

4. Brush the fruits all over with the jellied cranberry sauce and sprinkle with mixed spice.

5. Place carefully on a hot barbecue, turning and brushing the kebabs frequently with the jellied cranberry sauce and sprinkling with mixed spice as necessary.

6. Cook for just long enough to warm the fruits. Serve as an accompaniment to all barbecued meals or as a sweet course.

Raspberry Turnovers

Makes 12

Flavourful turnovers from central Europe, with a similar cottage cheese pastry to the one used in the Curried Onion Patties (page 46).

4oz (125g) cottage cheese
4oz (125g) butter, taken from the refrigerator
  and coarsely grated
4oz (125g) plain flour, sifted
1 level tsp cinnamon
12 level tsps raspberry jam
milk for brushing
1½ level tbsps castor sugar

1. Lightly grease a baking tray. Preheat oven to 220°C (425°F), gas mark 7.

2. Put cheese, butter, flour and cinnamon into a mixing bowl. Knead until smooth. Wrap and refrigerate for half an hour.

3. Roll out pastry thinly. Cut into 12 rounds with a 3½" (9cm) biscuit cutter.

4. Place 1 teaspoon of raspberry jam onto centre of each round.

5. Brush edges with milk then fold over to form semi-circles. Pinch edges firmly between finger and thumb to seal. Transfer to baking tray.

6. Make a small slit in each, brush with milk and sprinkle with sugar. Bake for 20 minutes just above oven centre.

7. Transfer to a wire rack and eat while still hot with cream or custard. Allow 2 per person.

Marmalade Turnovers

Makes 12

Follow previous recipe but use mixed spice instead of cinnamon and orange marmalade instead of raspberry jam.

American Style Apple Pie

Serves 6 to 8

American Apple Pie is different from our own in that the filling is more spicy and thickened with flour. This is a typical example.

Pastry
12oz (350g) plain flour
½ level tsp salt
1 level tsp finely grated lemon peel
3oz (75g) butter or margarine
3oz (75g) white cooking fat
3 tbsps cold water to mix

Filling
5oz (150g) light brown soft sugar
1½ level tbsp flour
1 level tsp cinnamon
½ level tsp mixed spice
1½lb (675g) cooking apples
1oz (25g) butter or margarine
2 level tsps castor sugar

1. Sift flour and salt into a bowl. Toss in lemon peel. Add fats and rub in finely then mix to a fairly soft dough with water. Wrap and refrigerate for 30 minutes.

2. Mix together sugar, flour and spices. Leave aside temporarily.

3. Peel, core and thinly slice apples. Toss in sugar mixture until evenly coated. Preheat oven to 220°C (425°F), gas mark 7.

4. On a lightly floured surface, roll out half the pastry and use to line a 10″ (25cm) greased pie plate.

5. Pile coated apples into dish then dot with butter or margarine.

6. Roll out remaining pastry to form a lid. Dampen edges and place on top of pie. Trim away any excess pastry and crimp edges to decorate. Make a slit in the lid to allow steam to escape.

7. Bake for 10 minutes. Lower heat to 180°C (350°F), gas mark 4 and continue baking for a further 35 to 40 minutes or until crust is pale gold.

8. Sprinkle with castor sugar and serve straight from the oven or when lukewarm. Accompany with whipped cream or vanilla ice cream.

Mulled Pears

Serves 6

A lovely simple party piece, unusually made with cider.

1 pint (575ml) medium sweet cider
2oz (50g) castor sugar
¼ level tsp cinnamon
¼ level tsp nutmeg
peel of ½ lemon
12 medium dessert pears

1. Place cider and sugar into a large pan. Stir over a low heat until sugar dissolves. Add cinnamon, nutmeg and strips of lemon peel.

2. Peel pears but leave whole. Add to liquid in pan, bring to the boil and cover.

3. Poach for 15 minutes then leave to cool in the liquid. Cover and refrigerate.

4. Serve chilled with pieces of cake or shop bought brandy snaps.

Double Crust Mixed Fruit Pie

Serves 6

A tender crust and fruity filling make this an outstanding pie for any occasion.

8oz (225g) plain flour
¼ level tsp salt
4oz (125g) white vegetable cooking fat
1 tsp white vinegar
5 tsps fresh orange juice
8oz (225g) cooking apples, peeled, cored, thinly sliced
8oz (225g) ripe dessert pears, peeled, cored and cut
   into small cubes
3oz (75g) light brown soft sugar
½ level tsp cinnamon
½ level tsp ginger
1 level tbsp cornflour
1 level tsp castor sugar

1. Preheat oven to 220°C (425°F), gas mark 7.

2. Sift flour and salt into a bowl. Add fat and rub in finely.

3. Using a fork, mix to a stiff dough with the vinegar and orange juice.

4. Turn out onto a lightly floured surface and knead quickly until smooth. Divide into 2 pieces. Roll out 1 piece and use to line an 8″ (20cm) pie plate.

5. Toss apples and pears in sugar, cinnamon and ginger. Stir in the cornflour then pile fruit into centre of pastry.

6. Roll out remaining pastry to form a lid. Dampen edges. Press on top of apples then pinch edges of pastry well together to seal. Brush top with water, sprinkle with castor sugar and make a slit in the centre to allow steam to escape.

7. Bake for 15 minutes. Reduce temperature to 180°C (350°F), gas mark 4 and bake for a further 30 minutes or until a warm gold.

8. Cut into portions and serve hot or warm with custard or cream.

Tropical Fruit Salad

Serves 4 to 6

An exotic fruit salad for sophisticated palates.

½ pint (275ml) raspberry juice
3oz (75g) castor sugar
12oz (350g) Ogen or honeydew melon, cut into
  ½" (1.25cm) cubes
10oz (275g) pineapple flesh, cut into
  ½" (1.25cm) cubes
1 8oz (225g) persimmon, peeled and cut into
  ¼" (5mm) cubes
2 kiwi fruit, peeled and thinly sliced
¼ level tsp allspice

1. Place raspberry juice and sugar into a small pan and stand over a low heat. Dissolve sugar, bring to the boil and boil rapidly for 5 minutes.

2. Remove from heat. Stir in fruit and allspice. Cover and leave until cold. Transfer to a glass dish. Cover with clingfilm and chill several hours before serving.

Tutti Frutti Pudding

Serves 4 to 6

A warmly-flavoured steamed pudding, sweetened with honey. It is 'quick mix' and takes just a few minutes.

3oz (75g) easy cream margarine
4oz (125g) clear honey
2 Grade 3 eggs
6oz (175g) wholemeal flour
1 tsp baking powder
1 level tsp allspice
2oz (50g) glacé cherries, quartered
2oz (50g) mixed chopped peel
2oz (50g) chocolate dots
1oz (25g) hazelnuts, coarsely chopped
1oz (25g) walnuts, coarsely chopped

1. Lightly grease a 2 pint (1.2 litre) pudding basin.

2. Place all pudding ingredients together into a mixing bowl and beat hard for 2 minutes when mixture should be well-combined and soft.

3. Transfer the mixture to prepared basin and level the surface.

4. Cover securely with greased foil and place in a large saucepan.

5. Add sufficient water to come halfway up the sides of the basin. Cover pan with lid and simmer for 1½ to 2 hours, topping up with extra boiling water every so often to keep up the level.

6. Turn out onto a warm plate and serve with white sauce sweetened with honey and flavoured with seeds from 2 opened-out cardamom pods.

CAKES AND BAKES

Cheese and Mustard Scone Round

Makes 8 Triangles

A handsome classic, brought bang-up-to-date with its topping of sesame seeds.

4oz (125g) wholemeal flour
4oz (125g) plain flour
4 level tsps baking powder ⎱ *Sifted*
½ level tsp powder mustard ⎰
½ level tsp salt
2oz (50g) butter or margarine, softened
2oz (50g) Cheddar cheese, grated
¼ pint (150ml) milk
extra milk to glaze
1 level tbsp sesame seeds

1. Grease a baking tray. Preheat oven to 220°C (425°F), gas mark 7.

2. Put flours, baking powder, mustard and salt into a bowl. Add butter or margarine and rub in finely. Toss in cheese then, using a fork, work to a soft dough with milk.

3. Turn out onto a lightly floured surface and knead briefly until smooth. Pat into a 1" (25cm) thick round and transfer to baking tray. Mark into 8 wedges with the back of a knife.

4. Brush with milk and sprinkle with sesame seeds. Bake just above oven centre for 20 minutes or until well-risen and golden brown.

5. Leave until lukewarm then break into triangles. Split each apart and spread with butter, margarine or low fat cream cheese. Accompany with salad.

Sesame Seed Cake

Makes a 2lb (900g) loaf

An easy savoury loaf, best sliced and spread with butter or margarine.

12oz (350g) self-raising flour
1 level tsp Rogan Josh curry powder
½ level tsp salt
5oz (150g) butter or margarine, softened
4oz (125g) Cheddar cheese, grated
4 level tbsps sesame seeds, toasted
2 Grade 3 eggs
8 tbsps milk

1. Grease and line a 2lb (900g) loaf tin. Preheat oven to 180°C (350°F), gas mark 4.

2. Sift flour, curry powder and salt into a bowl. Add butter or margarine and rub in until mixture resembles fine breadcrumbs. Toss in cheese and sesame seeds.

3. Lightly beat eggs and milk. Stir into flour mixture with a fork until thoroughly blended.

4. Spoon into prepared tin, level surface, and bake in oven centre for 1¼ hours or until well-risen and golden brown.

5. Allow to cool in tin for 10 minutes before turning out onto a wire rack. Store airtight when cold.

Curried Cheese Squares

Makes 16

Appetizing for picnics with a bowl of fresh and crisp green salad and whole baby tomatoes.

12oz (350g) wholemeal flour
1 level tbsp Madras curry powder
1 level tsp salt
6oz (175g) mixture of margarine and white
*   vegetable cooking fat*
4 tbsps cold water
8oz (225g) Cheddar cheese, grated
2 level tsps desiccated coconut, toasted
1 level tsp powder mustard
2 Grade 3 eggs, beaten
milk to glaze
2 level tsps paprika

1. Lightly grease a large baking tray. Preheat oven to 200°C (400°F), gas mark 6.

2. Place flour in a bowl. Sift in curry powder and salt. Add fats and rub in finely. Using a fork, mix to a stiff dough with water.

3. Turn out onto a lightly floured surface and knead briefly until smooth. Divide pastry into 2 equal portions and roll both out into 12″ × 9″ (30 × 23cm) rectangles. Place one of the rectangles onto prepared baking tray.

4. Mix together cheese, coconut, mustard and eggs. Spread evenly over pastry to within ½″ (1.25cm) of edges. Brush edges with milk. Place second piece of pastry on top to form a lid and seal by pressing edges well together. Make a series of slits in the top.

5. Brush with milk and sprinkle with paprika. Bake just above oven centre for 35 minutes and allow to cool on the tray before slicing into 16 bars. Serve warm or cold.

Curried Caraway Biscuits

Makes 44

Cocktail biscuits which are a personal favourite. Well worth having on tap for parties.

8oz (225g) plain flour
1 level tbsp Madras curry powder
½ level tsp salt
½ level tsp paprika
5oz (150g) butter or margarine, softened
2oz (50g) Cheddar cheese, finely grated
1 Grade 2 egg, beaten
2 tsps milk
4 level tsps caraway seeds

1. Grease 3 baking trays. Preheat oven to 190°C (375°F), gas mark 5.

2. Sift flour, curry powder, salt and paprika into a bowl. Add butter or margarine and rub in finely. Toss in the cheese.

3. Add 2 tablespoons of beaten egg and mix to a stiff dough with a fork. Turn out onto a lightly floured surface and knead quickly until smooth.

4. Roll out thinly then cut into 24 rounds with a 2″ (5cm) biscuit cutter, re-rolling and re-cutting trimmings to make the required number.

5. Transfer to prepared trays. Lightly whisk remaining egg with milk and brush over biscuits. Sprinkle with caraway seeds.

6. Bake towards top of oven for 13 to 15 minutes or until a warm golden colour, reversing position of trays halfway through baking.

7. Remove from oven and allow to cool for 2 to 3 minutes before transferring to a wire rack. Store airtight when cold.

Bacon Bars

Makes 18

Popular for weekends in the summer, these appetizing Bacon Bars go down well with coleslaw salad and apple juice.

12oz (350g) plain flour
1 level tbsp turmeric
1 level tsp salt
6oz (175g) mixture of margarine and white
*   vegetable cooking fat*
4 tbsps cold water
12oz (350g) unsmoked streaky bacon, de-rinded
*   and coarsely chopped*
6oz (175g) onions, peeled and coarsely chopped
2oz (50g) fresh, white breadcrumbs
1 Grade 3 egg, beaten
1 level tsp powder mustard
½ level tsp savory
¼ level tsp salt
pepper
milk for brushing

1. Lightly grease a large baking tray. Preheat oven to 200°C (400°F), gas mark 6.

2. Sift flour, turmeric and salt into a bowl. Add fats and rub in finely. Using a fork, mix to a stiff dough with water. Turn out onto a lightly floured surface and knead briefly until smooth.

3. Divide pastry in half and roll each into a 12″ × 9″ (32 × 23cm) rectangle. Cover loosely with clingfilm and leave aside temporarily.

4. Mince bacon and onions then stir in breadcrumbs, egg, mustard, savory, salt and pepper to taste. Place one pastry rectangle onto prepared baking tray.

5. Cover with bacon mixture to within ½″ (1.25cm) of edges. Brush with water then cover with the second pastry rectangle. Press edges well together to seal and prick all over with a fork.

6. Brush with milk and bake just above oven centre for 45 minutes. Cool to lukewarm in tin, cut into 18 pieces and lift out onto a wire cooling rack. Eat while warm or hot.

Fried Onion and Paprika Loaf

Makes a 1lb (450g) loaf

Designed for the buffet table, this goes very well with all grilled foods, in addition to salads and portions of cold chicken.

1 tbsp salad oil
8oz (225g) onions, peeled and finely chopped
8oz (225g) self raising flour
½ level tsp salt
1 level tsp paprika
3oz (75g) butter or margarine, softened
1 Grade 3 egg
5 tbsps milk

1. Grease and line a 1lb (450g) loaf tin. Preheat oven to 180°C (350°F), gas mark 4.

2. Heat oil. Add onions and fry until light golden brown, allowing about 10 minutes. Leave to cool.

3. Sift flour, salt and paprika into a bowl. Add fat and rub in until mixture resembles fine breadcrumbs. Toss in the fried onions.

4. Lightly beat egg and milk. Using a fork, stir into flour mixture until thoroughly blended. Spoon smoothly into prepared tin and bake in oven centre for 1¼ hours or until well-risen and golden.

5. Allow to cool in the tin for 10 minutes before turning out onto a wire rack. Store airtight when cold.

Curried Scones

Makes 9

A useful contribution for high tea or supper. Also stylish.

8oz (225g) self-raising flour
1 level tsp mild curry powder
½ level tsp salt
¼ level tsp ground coriander
2oz (50g) butter or margarine, softened
¼ pint (150ml) milk
extra milk for brushing

1. Grease a baking tray. Preheat oven to 230°C (450°F), gas mark 8.

2. Sift flour, curry powder, salt and coriander into a bowl. Add butter or margarine and rub in finely. Pour in milk in one go and stir to a soft dough with a fork.

3. Turn out onto a lightly floured surface and knead briefly until smooth.

4. Roll out to ½" (1.25cm) in thickness then cut into 9 rounds with a 2½" (6.5cm) biscuit cutter.

5. Place on prepared tray and brush tops with a little milk. Bake just above oven centre for 10 minutes or until well-risen and golden brown.

6. Transfer to a wire rack and leave to cool. Split apart before serving and eat buttered.

Tip
If possible, make and eat on the same day. If not, re-heat until just warm before serving.

Three Layer Cheese Triangles

Makes 8

Savoury 'biscuits' with a difference, based on three assorted cheeses.

8oz (225g) plain flour
½ level tsp powder mustard
¼ level tsp salt
¼ level tsp paprika
4oz (125g) mixture of butter or margarine and
    white vegetable cooking fat
approximately 4 tbsps cold water
4oz (125g) Cheddar cheese, finely grated
4oz (125g) Brie cheese, thinly sliced
3oz (75g) grated Parmesan cheese
milk for brushing

1. Lightly grease an 8" (20cm) sandwich tin. Preheat oven to 220°C (425°F), gas mark 7.

2. Sift flour, mustard, salt and paprika into a bowl. Add fats and rub in finely. Using a fork, mix to a stiff dough with water.

3. Turn out onto a floured surface and knead lightly until smooth.

4. Divide pastry in half. Roll out one half and press over base of tin.

5. Sprinkle grated cheese over pastry, arrange slices of Brie on top then shower with the Parmesan cheese. Press down lightly with fingertips.

6. Roll our remaining pastry and use to cover cheese. Prick top with a fork and brush with milk. Bake for 10 minutes. Reduce heat to 190°C (375°F), gas mark 5. Cook for a further 15 minutes.

7. Cut into 8 triangles. Allow to cool in the tin then carefully transfer to a wire cooling rack. Store airtight when cold.

Wholemeal Fig and Apricot Slices

Makes 12

Packed with fibre, these slices have a beautifully mellow flavour and appealing textures.

Filling
6oz (175g) dried apricots, soaked overnight in
   1 pint (575ml) water
4oz (125g) dried figs
¼ pint (150ml) apple juice
6 juniper berries, crushed
1 level tsp grated orange peel
2oz (50g) light brown soft sugar

Pastry
8oz (225g) wholemeal flour
2 level tsps baking powder
4oz (125g) butter or margarine
2oz (50g) light brown soft sugar
4 tbsps milk

Topping
4oz (125g) brown breadcrumbs
2oz (50g) light brown soft sugar
2oz (50g) butter or margarine, melted
½ level tsp mixed spice

1. Drain apricots and coarsely chop. Chop figs. Place both in a pan with apple juice, crushed juniper berries and orange peel. Bring to the boil, cover pan and simmer for 25 minutes until thick and pulpy. Stir in sugar and leave until cold.

2. Lightly grease a 12½″ × 9″ (32 × 23cm) Swiss roll tin. Preheat oven to 190°C (375°F), gas mark 5.

3. For pastry, place flour in a bowl. Sift in baking powder. Add butter or margarine and rub in finely. Toss in sugar then, using a fork, mix to a stiff dough with milk.

4. Turn pastry out onto a lightly floured surface and knead quickly until smooth. Roll out and use to line base and sides of Swiss roll tin. Spread cold filling mixture over pastry.

5. For topping, mix breadcrumbs with remaining ingredients and sprinkle over the filling.

6. Bake just above oven centre for 35 minutes. Cut into 12 slices and leave to cool in the tin. Lift out onto a wire rack and leave until cold before eating. Store airtight.

Spritz Biscuits

Makes 14

Crisp, elegant and typically Continental biscuits for important occasions.

6oz (175g) butter, softened (not margarine)
3oz (75g) icing sugar
½ level tsp allspice
½ tsp vanilla essence
6oz (175g) plain flour

1. Grease one large baking tray. Preheat oven to 160°C (325°F), gas mark 3.

2. Place butter in a bowl. Sift in icing sugar and allspice. Add essence then beat until light and fluffy.

3. Sift in flour and fork ingredients together until thoroughly combined.

4. Spoon mixture into a large piping bag fitted with a ½″ (1.25cm) fluted nozzle. Pipe 14 'S' shapes onto tray, leaving room between each as the biscuits spread out and flatten.

5. Bake for 20 minutes. Leave on tray for 5 minutes before carefully transferring to a wire cooling rack. Store airtight when cold.

Chocolate Dot Ginger Cookies

Makes 20

One of the most popular biscuits ever, this time laced with ginger.

4oz (125g) butter, softened (do not use margarine)
2oz (50g) castor sugar
2oz (50g) walnuts, chopped
2oz (50g) plain chocolate dots
1oz (25g) stem ginger, finely chopped
4oz (125g) plain flour
½ level tsp ground ginger

1. Grease 2 baking trays. Preheat oven to 190°C (375°F), gas mark 5.

2. Cream butter and sugar together until light and fluffy.

3. Stir in nuts, chocolate dots and chopped ginger. Sift in flour and ground ginger. Using a fork, stir to form a fairly soft dough.

4. Place 20 tablespoons of mixture, well apart, onto prepared baking trays.

5. Bake just above oven centre for 15 to 20 minutes. Leave on baking trays for 2 minutes before carefully transferring to wire cooling rack.

6. Store airtight when completely cold.

Raisin Apple Bars

Makes 14

Autumn is the time of year to collect windfalls and make these spicy apple bars with their mellow, fruity flavour.

10oz (275g) plain flour
2 level tsps bicarbonate of soda
2 level tsps cinnamon
¼ level tsp allspice
4oz (125g) butter or margarine, softened
1oz (25g) light brown soft sugar
6oz (175g) golden syrup
2 Grade 3 eggs
2 tsps vanilla essence
1¼lb (575g) cooking apples, peeled, cored,
* finely chopped*
5oz (150g) raisins
2oz (50g) chopped walnuts

1. Line a 12″ × 9″ (32 × 23cm) roasting tin with non-stick parchment paper. Preheat oven to 180°C (350°F), gas mark 4.

2. Sift flour, bicarbonate of soda, cinnamon and allspice into a bowl.

3. In separate bowl, cream butter or margarine until smooth and soft. Beat in sugar and golden syrup. Add eggs and essence and beat until just incorporated.

4. Fold sifted dry ingredients, chopped apples and raisins alternately into egg mixture.

5. Spoon evenly into prepared tin and sprinkle with chopped nuts.

6. Bake for 35 to 40 minutes or until a warm gold. Leave to cool in the tin before cutting into 14 bars.

7. Remove to a wire rack when lukewarm then leave until cold before storing airtight.

Scandinavian Tea Cakes

Makes 2

Well-loved in the north, these are light and fragrantly flavoured cakes which go best with coffee and hot chocolate.

2 level tbsps dried yeast
2 level tsps castor sugar
¼ pint (150ml) warm water
2lb (900g) strong plain white flour
2 level tsps salt
6oz (175g) castor sugar
1 level tbsp ground cardamom
4oz (125g) butter or margarine, softened
¾ pint (450ml) milk
1 Grade 4 egg, beaten
1oz (25g) castor sugar
1oz (25g) flaked almonds

1. Sprinkle yeast and sugar onto water. Stand in a warm place for 15 to 20 minutes until frothy.

2. Sift flour, salt, sugar and cardamom into a bowl. Add butter or margarine and rub in finely.

3. Make a well in the centre. Add yeast liquid and milk then mix to a soft dough with fingertips. Turn out and knead for 8 to 10 minutes until it is smooth, elastic and no longer sticky.

4. Place in an oiled bowl. Cover loosely with oiled clingfilm and leave to rise in a warm place until dough doubles in size — 1 to 1½ hours.

5. Lightly grease 2 baking trays. Preheat oven to 200°C (400°F), gas mark 6.

6. Re-knead dough until smooth on floured surface then divide in half. Cut each half into 3 and roll into 9″ (23cm) long strips. Plait in threes, coil each into a ring on baking trays and join ends by pinching together.

7. Cover loosely with oiled clingfilm and leave to rise in the warm until double in size.

8. Brush each with egg then sprinkle with sugar and almonds. Bake for 30 minutes in oven set to 200°C (400°F), gas mark 6. Reverse position of trays halfway through baking.

9. Leave cakes on trays for 10 minutes then transfer to a wire rack to cool. Eat freshly made, when just cold.

Coconut and Coriander Dropped Scones

Makes 26 to 30

Warming little savoury scones for tea or supper.

8oz (225g) self-raising flour
½ level tsp salt
1oz (25g) desiccated coconut
1 level tbsp chopped fresh coriander
1 Grade 3 egg
½ pint (275ml) milk
1oz (25g) melted butter or margarine

1. Sift flour and salt into a bowl. Toss in coconut and coriander.

2. Add egg and half the milk. Beat to a smooth batter then gently stir in remaining milk.

3. Brush a large frying pan with melted butter or margarine. Heat until hot.

4. Drop in tablespoons of the scone mixture. Cook until bubbles show on the surface, about 1½ to 2 minutes.

5. Turn over and cook for a further 2 minutes. Remove to a dish, lined with a clean cloth. Serve the scones hot with butter or margarine and cheese to taste.

Wholemeal Chocolate Nut Cookies

Makes 26

High-fibre biscuits with chocolate dots and peanuts for luxury touches.

4oz (125g) butter or margarine, softened
3oz (75g) golden syrup
1 tsp vanilla essence
4oz (125g) wholemeal flour
4 level tbsps bran
2oz (50g) plain chocolate dots
1oz (25g) chopped unsalted peanuts

1. Grease 2 baking trays. Preheat oven to 160°C (325°F), gas mark 3.

2. Cream butter or margarine, syrup and essence together until pale in colour and light in texture.

3. Beat in flour and bran. Stir in chocolate dots and nuts then draw mixture together with a fork.

4. Place between 2 sheets of non-stick parchment paper. Roll out to ⅛″ (3mm) in thickness. Lay flat on a baking tray and place in the freezer for 10 minutes.

5. Remove top piece of non-stick paper then cut into rounds with a 2″ (5cm) biscuit cutter. Transfer to prepared trays.

6. Re-roll trimmings between paper, return to freezer for a further 5 minutes then cut into more rounds. Add to others on trays.

7. Bake towards top of oven for 12 minutes, reversing position of trays halfway through baking.

8. Leave on trays for 1 minute before transferring to a wire rack to cool. Store airtight when cold.

Lemon Curd and Almond Tarts

Makes 12

Luxurious little tarts, filled with lemon curd and an almond meringue.

Pastry
4oz (125g) plain flour
2oz (50g) butter or margarine, softened
1 level tbsp castor sugar
1 Grade 3 egg yolk
cold water to mix

Filling
4 level tbsps lemon curd
1 Grade 3 egg white
2oz (50g) castor sugar
3 level tbsps ground almonds
¼ tsp almond essence
3 level tbsps flaked almonds

1. Set oven to 180°C (350°F), gas mark 4. For pastry, sift flour into a bowl. Add butter or margarine and rub in finely.

2. Toss in sugar then, using a fork, mix to a stiff paste with egg yolk and a little cold water.

3. Roll out on a lightly floured surface and cut into 12 rounds with a 3½″ (9cm) biscuit cutter. Use to line 12 lightly greased bun tins.

4. Spoon equal amounts of lemon curd into each. Stiffly beat egg white then stir in the sugar, ground almonds and essence. Spoon into pastry cases, completely covering the curd. Sprinkle flaked almonds on top.

5. Bake just above oven centre for 20 to 25 minutes or until a warm golden colour.

6. Remove from oven, cool for 5 minutes in tins then lift out onto a wire cooling rack. Eat when cold.

Clementine Fruit Cake

Makes an 8″ (20cm) cake

A fine weekender cake for family and friends.

8oz (225g) wholemeal flour
2 level tsps mixed spice
1 level tsp baking powder
6oz (175g) butter or block margarine, softened
5oz (150g) light brown soft sugar
1 level tbsp golden syrup
finely grated peel of 1 clementine
3 Grade 3 eggs
12oz (350g) sultanas
4oz (125g) glacé cherries, halved, washed, dried
2oz (50g) walnuts, finely ground in a blender or
     food processor
2 tbsps milk

1. Grease and line an 8″ (20cm) round cake tin. Preheat oven to 150°C (300°F), gas mark 2.

2. Place flour in a bowl. Sift in spice and baking powder.

3. In separate bowl, cream butter or margarine, sugar, syrup and clementine peel until light and fluffy.

4. Beat in eggs, one at a time, adding a tablespoon of sifted dry ingredients with each.

5. Stir in sultanas, cherries and walnuts then, using a large metal spoon, fold in dry ingredients with milk.

6. Spoon into prepared tin. Level top with a knife then bake in oven centre for 2½ hours.

7. Leave in tin for 30 minutes before turning out onto a wire rack to cool. Store airtight when cold.

Spicy Cherry Cake

Makes a 1lb (450g) loaf cake

An unusual cherry cake with an attractive speckled texture.

8oz (225g) wholemeal flour
2 level tsps baking powder
1 level tsp mixed spice
4oz (125g) butter or block margarine, softened
4oz (125g) light brown soft sugar
4oz (125g) glacé cherries, washed, dried,
     finely chopped
1 Grade 3 egg
½ tsp vanilla essence
5 tbsps milk

1. Grease and line a 1lb (450g) loaf tin. Preheat oven to 180°C (350°F), gas mark 4.

2. Place flour in a bowl. Sift in baking powder and mixed spice.

3. Add butter or margarine and rub in until mixture resembles fine breadcrumbs. Toss in sugar and cherries.

4. Whisk together egg, essence and milk. Add to flour mixture then fork-stir thoroughly, without beating, until well-combined.

5. Spread evenly into prepared tin and bake for 1 to 1¼ hours in oven centre until well-risen and golden. Allow to cool in tin for 15 minutes before turning out onto a wire cooling rack. Store airtight when cold.

Date and Oat Cakes

Makes 18

Bar-shaped cakes which are sweet, rich and, I have to admit, calorie-laden!

3oz (75g) plain flour
½ level tsp bicarbonate of soda
1 level tsp cinnamon
¼ level tsp allspice
8fl oz (225ml) boiling water
7oz (200g) porridge oats
1lb (450g) butter or margarine, melted
12oz (350g) light brown soft sugar
6oz (175g) chopped walnuts
2 Grade 2 eggs, beaten
12oz (350g) dates, fairly finely chopped

1. Preheat oven to 180°C (350°F), gas mark 4. Grease and line an 11½″ × 9½″ (29 × 24cm) Swiss roll tin.

2. Sift flour, bicarbonate of soda, cinnamon and allspice into a bowl. Keep aside temporarily.

3. Pour boiling water onto oats. Stir in melted butter or margarine, sugar, nuts, eggs and dates. Using a fork, thoroughly mix in the dry ingredients.

4. Spread into prepared tin and bake for 45 minutes or until golden brown. Cool in tin then cut into 18 pieces.

5. Remove carefully to a wire rack then leave until cold. Store airtight.

Swede Cup Cakes

Makes 24

High-protein tofu (bean curd), swede, golden syrup and salad oil have been combined in this recipe to make tender little cakes which are pleasing to eat and healthy into the bargain.

2 Grade 3 eggs
6oz (175g) golden syrup
4fl oz (125ml) vegetable oil
6oz (175g) firm tofu, drained
2 level tsps bicarbonate of soda
2 level tsps finely grated lemon peel
2 tsps lemon juice
8oz (225g) wholemeal flour
4oz (125g) uncooked swede, peeled and finely grated
4oz (125g) chopped mixed nuts

1. Stand 24 paper cake cases in 24 ungreased bun tins. Preheat oven to 160°C (325°F), gas mark 3.

2. Place eggs, syrup, oil, tofu, bicarbonate of soda, lemon peel and juice into a food processor. Blend until smooth.

3. Transfer mixture to a bowl. Stir in flour, swede and nuts.

4. Divide mixture evenly between paper cake cases. Bake towards top of oven for 25 minutes, reversing position of trays halfway through baking.

5. Transfer to a wire rack and leave until cold before eating. Store airtight.

Novice's Christmas Cake

Makes an 8" (20cm) cake

A splendid contribution to the festive season is this moist and fruit-laden cake made with oil instead of the more customary butter or margarine.

8oz (225g) plain flour
½ level tsp baking powder
¼ level tsp bicarbonate of soda
¼ level tsp mixed spice
2 Grade 2 eggs
6oz (175g) castor sugar
6fl oz (175ml) salad oil (not olive)
1 level tbsp black treacle
½ tsp vanilla essence
1lb (450g) mixed dried fruits (currants, sultanas, raisins and dates)
2oz (50g) chopped walnuts

1. Grease and line an 8" (20cm) round cake tin. Preheat oven to 150°C (300°F), gas mark 2.

2. Sift flour, baking powder, bicarbonate of soda and spice into a bowl.

3. In separate bowl, beat eggs and sugar until just combined. Gradually whisk in oil, followed by treacle and essence.

4. Stir in fruit, nuts and sifted dry ingredients.

5. Pour into cake tin and bake for 2 hours in oven centre. Leave to stand for 30 minutes before turning out onto a wire cooling rack.

6. Remove lining paper when cake is completely cold. Wrap in aluminium foil and store in the cool. Leave cake for one week before decorating and cutting.

Wholemeal Honey Spice Cake

Makes one 6" (15cm) cake

A quality cake made with brown flour and sweetened with both sugar and honey.

8oz (225g) wholemeal flour
3 level tsps baking powder
1 level tsp mixed spice
½ level tsp cinnamon
4oz (125g) butter or margarine, softened
2oz (50g) light brown soft sugar
3 level tbsps clear honey
1 Grade 3 egg
5 tbsps milk

1. Grease and line a 6" (15cm) round cake tin. Preheat oven to 180°C (350°F), gas mark 4.

2. Place flour in a bowl. Sift in baking powder and spices. Add butter or margarine and rub in finely until mixture resembles fine breadcrumbs. Toss in sugar.

3. Whisk together honey, egg and milk. Add to flour mixture and stir thoroughly with a fork until well-combined.

4. Transfer evenly to prepared tin and bake for 1 to 1¼ hours in oven centre or until cake is well-risen and golden brown.

5. Leave in tin for 10 minutes before turning out onto a wire rack. Store airtight when completely cold.

PRESERVES

Toffee Apple Jam

Makes about 5lbs (2.25kg)

An aromatic and deep golden brown jam, unique in my experience.

6oz (175g) kiwi fruit, peeled and sliced
1¼lb (575g) persimmons (3 medium), each cut into eighths
1lb (450g) cooking apples, peeled, cored, sliced
1¾lb (750g) pineapple, peeled and chopped
1 pint (575ml) water
3" (7.5cm) length of cinnamon stick
3½lb (1.5kg) demerara sugar

1. Put fruit and water into a large saucepan with cinnamon stick. Bring to boil, stirring.

2. Lower heat and cover. Simmer gently for about 40 minutes or until fruit is very soft. Remove cinnamon stick and discard.

3. Add sugar and stir until dissolved. Increase heat and boil fairly briskly until setting point is reached.

4. Stir frequently. To test, use a preserving thermometer which should register 220°F (140°C). Alternatively, pour a little jam onto a cold saucer and leave for 2 minutes in the cool. If a skin forms on top which wrinkles when touched, the jam is ready. If not, continue to cook until setting point is reached, checking every few minutes.

5. Remove scum, leave jam to cool for 10 minutes then pot and cover. Store in a cool, dark and dry cupboard.

Apple, Pineapple and Ginger Jam

Makes 5lbs (2.25kg)

A fine example of mixing two autumnal fruits and spicing them with stem ginger.

2lbs (900g) cooking apples, peeled, cored, thinly sliced
2½lbs (1.25kg) pineapple, peeled and finely chopped
1½ pints (900ml) water
3lbs (1.5kg) light brown soft sugar
8oz (225g) finely chopped preserved ginger
4 tbsps preserved ginger syrup
finely grated peel and juice of 3 medium lemons

1. Tie apple peel and cores in a piece of muslin or other soft, clean cloth. Place in a large pan with sliced apples, pineapple and water. Bring to the boil and simmer, uncovered, for 30 minutes.

2. Remove muslin bag from pan and discard. Stir sugar into fruit mixture followed by ginger, ginger syrup, lemon peel and juice.

3. Stir until sugar is dissolved. Bring to the boil and cook fairly rapidly until setting point is reached. To test, see Toffee Apple Jam.

4. Take pan off heat and remove scum. Cool for 10 minutes then pot and cover. Store in a cool, dark and dry cupboard.

Cranberry, Apple and Nut Jam

Makes 2½lbs (1.25kg)

An old favourite which is sweet-sour, brilliantly coloured and enchanced by nuts.

1lb (450g) cooking apples, peeled, quartered,
*   coarsely chopped*
8oz (225g) fresh cranberries, washed
piece of cinnamon stick measuring 2" (5cm)
4 tbsps water
finely grated peel and chopped pulp of
*   1 medium orange*
1oz (25g) pecan nuts or walnuts, coarsely chopped
1½lb (675g) granulated sugar

1. Place apples, cranberries, cinnamon stick and water into a large saucepan. Bring to the boil and simmer, uncovered, until pulpy. Allow between 15 and 25 minutes. Stir occasionally.

2. Remove cinnamon stick. Add orange peel and pulp, nuts and sugar. Stir until sugar dissolves.

3. Bring to the boil and boil fairly rapidly for 15 to 20 minutes until setting point is reached. To test, see Toffee Apple Jam.

4. Remove scum then cool jam for 10 minutes. Pot and cover. Store in a cool, dark and dry cupboard.

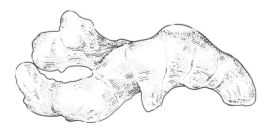

Spicy Pineapple and Apple Chutney

Makes 6lbs (2.75kg)

A fine chutney to serve with curries, egg dishes and cold meats.

2lbs (900g) cooking apples, peeled, cored, sliced
2½lbs (1.25kg) pineapple, peeled and fairly
*   finely chopped*
2lbs (900g) onions, peeled and coarsely chopped
1lb (450g) sultanas
2 pints (1.2 litres) malt vinegar
1½lbs (675g) light brown soft sugar
1½ level tsp salt
2 level tsps mixed spice
2 level tsps ground ginger
2 level tsps cinnamon
1 level tbsp pickling spice
6 cloves   }   Tied in a piece
1 bay leaf   }   of clean cloth

1. Mince apples, pineapple and onions. Place in a large pan with sultanas and 1 pint (575ml) vinegar. Bring to the boil and simmer, uncovered, for 30 minutes. Stir occasionally.

2. Add remaining ingredients and stir until sugar is dissolved. Cook, uncovered, until pulpy. Allow about 1¼ to 1½ hours and stir occasionally.

3. Cool chutney to lukewarm then pot and cover. Store in a cool, dark and dry cupboard.

ODDS AND ENDS

High Fibre Coating Mix

Use this coating for fish, meat or poultry. Alternatively, sprinkle over dishes such as cauliflower cheese, casseroles with a white sauce, shepherd's pie and even creamed potato.

3oz (75g) sesame seeds, toasted under the grill
3 level tbsps bran, toasted under the grill
5oz (150g) wholemeal flour
1 level tsp paprika
2 level tsps parsley flakes
2 level tsps poultry seasoning
1 level tsp onion powder
¼ level tsp garlic granules

1. Coarsely grind sesame seeds in food processor or blender.

2. Mix with remaining ingredients.

3. Transfer to a polythene bag and tie securely. Store in the refrigerator or, if preferred, put into a screw-topped jar and keep in a dry, dark and cool cupboard.

Note
Storage time is about 2 to 3 months.

Sausagemeat and Apple Stuffing

An unusual stuffing for a medium-sized turkey or large chicken.

3oz (75g) onions, peeled and chopped
2oz (50g) butter or margarine, melted
4oz (125g) fresh brown breadcrumbs
1 level tbsp chopped parsley or fresh coriander
8oz (225g) apples, peeled, cored, chopped
12oz (350g) sausagemeat
3 tbsps dry sherry or stock
1 Grade 2 egg, beaten

1. Fry onions gently in the butter or margarine until pale gold.

2. Remove from heat. Stir in crumbs, parsley or coriander and apples.

3. Work in sausagemeat with sherry and gradual amounts of egg. Use as required.

Herb Butters

Slightly salted lactic butter lends itself perfectly to making fresh herb butters. Cream the butter until it looks like stiffly whipped cream and then add the finely chopped herbs (see below). Place the mixture in greaseproof paper and roll it into a sausage shape. Leave in the refrigerator until firm then cut into slices as required to garnish cooked dishes.

Herb butters can be served in little pots for guests to spread on rolls or crispbread served with soup or cheese.

Parsley butter: Cream 3oz (75g) butter then add 1 teaspoon lemon juice and 1 level tablespoon chopped parsley. Serve with fried or grilled fish.

Mint butter: Cream 3oz (75g) butter then add 1 level tablespoon freshly chopped mint. Serve with lamb dishes or with plain omelettes.

Rosemary butter: Pick a sprig of fresh rosemary. Strip the spikey leaves off the stem and cut them finely. Add to 3oz (75g) creamed butter. This is particularly good with plain boiled spaghetti and macaroni.

Chive butter: Cream 3oz (75g) butter and add 1 teaspoon lemon juice and 1 tablespoon chopped fresh chives. Serve sliced with bacon steaks or chops, or spread it on biscuits for cocktail snacks.

Paprika butter: Cream 3oz (75g) butter, shape and cut into slices. Dip the slices in mild paprika and serve with fried chicken or beef steaks.

Curried butter: Cream 3oz (75g) butter and add a squeeze of lemon juice. Shape and cut into slices. Just before serving dip each slice in curry powder. Serve with fried fish or scrambled eggs.

Poultry Baste for Microwave Roasting

Brush this over chicken or turkey before microwaving for an attractive golden glaze.

1oz (25g) butter or margarine
1 tsp Worcestershire sauce
2 tsps tomato ketchup
1 level tsp paprika
½ level tsp garlic or onion salt

1. Melt butter or margarine.

2. Beat in rest of ingredients and use as required.

Mustard Glaze

Perfect for large pieces of gammon which have been boiled and de-rinded.

4 level tbsps golden syrup
2 level tbsps dark brown soft sugar
¼ level tsp powdered cloves
¼ level tsp cinnamon
2 level tsps mustard powder

1. Melt golden syrup gently in a saucepan.

2. Stir in all remaining ingredients.

3. Score gammon fat into diamonds. Brush thickly with baste. Brown for 15 minutes in a moderately hot oven set to 200°C (400°F), gas mark 6.

4. Brush with remaining baste and continue to bake for a further 15 minutes.

Seasoned Herb Crumbs

An appetizing coating for fish, poultry and lamb chops.

4oz (125g) wholemeal bread, weighed after crusts have been removed
1 level tsp mixed herbs
1 level tsp basil
1 level tsp thyme
1 level tsp parsley flakes
½ level tsp marjoram
½ level tsp rosemary
½ level tsp savory
½ level tsp celery seeds
½ level tsp fennel seeds
½ level tsp ground coriander
½ level tsp sage
½ level tsp turmeric
½ level tsp paprika
½ level tsp salt
¼ level tsp garlic granules

1. Turn bread into very fine crumbs in a blender or food processor.
2. Add remaining ingredients and process until thoroughly combined.
3. Store as the High Fibre Coating Mix.

Parmesan Seasoned Herb Crumbs

Make as previous recipe but add 1oz (25g) finely grated Parmesan cheese with the herbs. It is useful for coating poultry, liver, veal and fish.

Chestnut Stuffing

A well-flavoured and interesting stuffing for chicken and turkey.

½oz (15g) butter or margarine
1 tsp salad oil
2oz (50g) onion, peeled and finely chopped
2oz (50g) parsley and thyme stuffing mix
1 15½oz (440g) can unsweetened chestnut purée
¼ pint (150ml) boiling water
1 garlic clove, peeled and crushed
finely grated peel of 1 large lemon
¼ level tsp salt

1. Heat butter or margarine and oil in a pan until sizzling. Add onion and fry over medium heat for 10 to 15 minutes until golden brown.
2. Add stuffing mix and fry for a further 5 minutes until crunchy.
3. Remove from heat. Stir in chestnut purée. Blend in all remaining ingredients. Mix well and cool. Use as required.

Elizabethan Glaze

An elegant glaze which adds its own note of subtlety to poultry.

2 tbsps freshly squeezed orange juice
4 level tbsps melted and sieved orange marmalade
1 level tbsp dark brown soft sugar
½ level tsp ground cloves

1. Mix ingredients well together.
2. Brush over chicken or turkey half an hour before it is ready.

Christmas Glaze

A rich, ruby red glaze designed for duck, goose and turkey.

3½fl oz (100ml) ruby port
4 level tbsps redcurrant jelly
1 level tsp finely grated orange peel
1 level tsp finely grated lemon peel
¼ levl tsp nutmeg

1. Put all the ingredients into a pan and stir over a low heat until jelly is melted.
2. Bring slowly to the boil. Boil gently for 10 minutes or until syrupy.
3. Brush over bird half an hour before it is ready.

Juniper and Orange Baste

A wonderfully subtle baste for poultry.

4 tbsps salad oil
4 tbsps dry white wine or dry cider
1 small onion (about 2oz or 50g), peeled and grated
½oz (15g) butter or margarine, melted
2 pinches of dried thyme
5 juniper berries, crushed
1 level tsps finely grated orange peel
1 or 2 grindings of black pepper
½ level tsp salt

1. Beat together oil and the wine or cider.
2. Mix in all remaining ingredients.
3. Pour over bird and baste frequently whilst roasting or grilling.

Cocoa Fudge

Makes 40 pieces

A super sweetmeat made without cooking. It keeps exceptionally well in the cool.

2oz (50g) butter or best margarine, softened
4oz (125g) skimmed milk powder (in powder form)
2oz (50g) cocoa powder
1 level tsp cinnamon
4oz (125g) golden syrup
1 tsp vanilla essence
2 tsps milk
3oz (75g) finely chopped mixed nuts

1. Cream butter in a basin until light in colour and consistency. Gradually beat in milk powder until mixture resembles breadcrumbs.
2. Sift in cocoa and cinnamon. Mix well.
3. Add syrup, essence and milk. Beat until thoroughly combined.
4. Knead in nuts and continue to knead until mixture is shiny.
5. Roll into 2 × 10″ (25cm) long rolls. Wrap in clingfilm or foil, put into a small tray and chill in the refrigerator for at least 30 minutes.
6. Unwrap rolls and cut each into 20 thick slices.

Mocha Fudge

Makes 40 pieces

Follow recipe for Cocoa Fudge but sift 2 level teaspoons instant coffee powder with cocoa and cinnamon.

INDEX